D0872242

Magicians and Illusionists

Other Books in the History Makers Series:

History MAKERS

Magicians and Illusionists

By Adam Woog

Lucent Books
P.O. Box 289011, San Diego, CA 92198-9011

Dedication
For Leah, my budding magician

Library of Congress Cataloging-in-Publication Data

Woog, Adam, 1953–
    Magicians and illusionists / by Adam Woog.
    Includes bibliographical references and index.
    Summary: Discusses the lives of eight famous magicians, including
Robert-Houdin, Herrman the Great, Kellar, Harry Houdini, Jasper
Maskelyne, David Copperfield, and Penn and Teller.
    ISBN 1–56006–573–7 (lib. bdg. : alk. paper)
    1. Magicians Biography Juvenile literature. [1. Magicians.]
I. Title. II. Series.
GV1545.A2W66   2000
793.8'092's—dc21   99–32345
[B]   CIP
                                                                  AC

Copyright 2000 by Lucent Books, Inc.
P.O. Box 289011, San Diego, California 92198-9011

Printed in the U.S.A.

CONTENTS

FOREWORD

The literary form most often referred to as "multiple biography" was perfected in the first century A.D. by Plutarch, a perceptive and talented moralist and historian who hailed from the small town of Chaeronea in central Greece. His most famous work, *Parallel Lives*, consists of a long series of biographies of noteworthy ancient Greek and Roman statesmen and military leaders. Frequently, Plutarch compares a famous Greek to a famous Roman, pointing out similarities in personality and achievements. These expertly constructed and very readable tracts provided later historians and others, including playwrights like Shakespeare, with priceless information about prominent ancient personages and also inspired new generations of writers to tackle the multiple biography genre.

The Lucent History Makers series proudly carries on the venerable tradition handed down from Plutarch. Each volume in the series consists of a set of six to eight biographies of important and influential historical figures who were linked together by a common factor. In *Rulers of Ancient Rome*, for example, all the figures were generals, consuls, or emperors of either the Roman Republic or Empire; while the subjects of *Fighters Against American Slavery*, though they lived in different places and times, all shared the same goal, namely the eradication of human servitude. Mindful that politicians and military leaders are not (and never have been) the only people who shape the course of history, the editors of the series have also included representatives from a wide range of endeavors, including scientists, artists, writers, philosophers, religious leaders, and sports figures.

Each book is intended to give a range of figures—some well known, others less known; some who made a great impact on history, others who made only a small impact. For instance, by making Columbus's initial voyage possible, Spain's Queen Isabella I, featured in *Women Leaders of Nations*, helped to open up the New World to exploration and exploitation by the European powers. Unarguably, therefore, she made a major contribution to a series of events that had momentous consequences for the entire world. By contrast, Catherine II, the eighteenth-century Russian queen, and Golda Meir, the modern Israeli prime minister, did not play roles of global impact; however, their policies and actions significantly influenced the historical development of both their own countries and their regional neighbors. Regardless of their relative importance in the greater historical scheme, all of the figures chronicled in the History Makers series made contributions to posterity; and their public achievements, as well as what is known about their private lives, are presented and evaluated in light of the most recent scholarship.

In addition, each volume in the series is documented and substantiated by a wide array of primary and secondary source quotations. The primary source quotes enliven the text by presenting eyewitness views of the times and culture in which each history maker lived; while the secondary source quotes, taken from the works of respected modern scholars, offer expert elaboration and/or critical commentary. Each quote is footnoted, demonstrating to the reader exactly where biographers find their information. The footnotes also provide the reader with the means of conducting additional research. Finally, to further guide and illuminate readers, each volume in the series features photographs, two bibliographies, and a comprehensive index.

The History Makers series provides both students engaged in research and more casual readers with informative, enlightening, and entertaining overviews of individuals from a variety of circumstances, professions, and backgrounds. No doubt all of them, whether loved or hated, benevolent or cruel, constructive or destructive, will remain endlessly fascinating to each new generation seeking to identify the forces that shaped their world.

Hocus Pocus!

Magic has fascinated men and women everywhere since ancient times. This powerful appeal has always stemmed from magic's connection with the occult.

Magicians in ancient times and in primitive societies derived their power over others by exploiting the belief that supernatural forces were at work in the world and that some humans could control those forces to perform seemingly impossible tasks, such as communicating with the dead or guaranteeing a bountiful crop.

White magic was that form of sorcery used for good, whereas black magic was used for evil. Whether white or black, the intent was always to create the *appearance* of harnessing the occult. Contemporary magician David Copperfield remarks, "When guys back in the caveman days figured out how to make a stick disappear, they didn't do it to make money, they did it to foster a belief in the supernatural or to be [perceived as] godlike, to deceive people and make them believe they had real powers. That's how my craft began." [1]

However, for most people today, the word *magic* has a very different connotation. It refers to a theatrical presentation, a show in which the audience knows that the magician only seems to be harnessing the powers of the occult. Audiences know they are being tricked but are willing to be deceived if it means seeing a thrilling show. Milbourne Christopher, a distinguished magician and author, remarks:

> Magicians are legitimate deceptionists [who] use their talents to create a world of fantasy. They challenge the mind, stimulate the imagination and offer a brief respite from worry and pressure. There is a vicarious thrill in seeing a fellow human cause roses to blossom and bloom in a few seconds or deal himself a winning poker hand purely for amusement. Even in this scientific age when one can pick up a telephone and talk to a friend across the ocean or enjoy a baseball game on a television screen as it is played a thousand miles away, audiences are still fascinated by the conjuring techniques which baffled their ancestors. [2]

The power of the magician derives from his or her ability to appear in control of supernatural forces.

Modern Magic

Magic, as the term is commonly used today, is thus far removed from its early aura of genuine control over supernatural forces. Although some modern magicians do claim a connection with the occult, generally speaking audiences today know that a magician's bag of tricks includes such prosaic techniques as sleight of hand, specially rigged equipment, and misdirection (the trick of drawing an audience's attention away from a particular area).

More accurate terms for magic today would probably be *legerdemain, conjuring,* or *illusion.* In everyday speech, however, these words are used interchangeably. A more recent term, *prestidigitation,* strictly speaking refers to the specific skill of manual dexterity.

Some historians of the field create a further distinction between magicians and illusionists. They would define a magician as someone who performs relatively simple tricks using relatively simple techniques. An illusionist, according to this distinction, specializes in presenting lavish, large-scale theatrical presentations. The contrast can be roughly illustrated by the difference between pulling a rabbit out of a hat versus making an elephant disappear.

The list of distinguished practitioners of modern magic and illusion is long. Many men (but, oddly, very few women) can legitimately vie for the title of "most famous" or "most innovative" of all the world's conjurors. However, it is possible to single out a handful of conjurors, both historical and contemporary, who have made significant contributions to this mysterious and fascinating art.

Robert-Houdin

Jean Eugene Robert-Houdin (1805–1871) is generally acknowledged by scholars of the field as "the Father of Modern Magic." Although, like many conjurors, he borrowed freely from other magicians, Robert-Houdin was important because of his refinements and improvements of illusions and performance styles. These changes influenced countless other magicians in future generations.

He was a genius at creating startling automata, or mechanical marvels, and presenting them onstage; he also integrated such then-new innovations as electricity into his show. He revolutionized the manner in which magic was presented onstage by simplifying his performances and using common props such as hats and tables without coverings. Furthermore, he gave to magic presentation an elegance and dignity often lacking of previous times.

Robert-Houdin also dispensed with the pretentious, Oriental-style flowing robes then common with European magicians. In their place, he wore simple evening clothes—the same as the men in his audience. Writer Kenneth Silverman summarizes Robert-Houdin's overall importance by noting his rejection of "the conventional pompous robes, flowing draperies, and bulky apparatus [of previous magicians, performing instead] in everyday clothes on a simplified stage using ordinary objects." [3]

Herrmann the Great

Alexander Herrmann (1843–1896), known professionally as Herrmann the Great, was the younger half of a pair of renowned magician brothers.

Herrmann's lasting fame stems partly from his striking appearance; he virtually invented the familiar "devilish" look that many magicians still use.

Another aspect of Herrmann's influence, which has lasted into the present day, was his genius for combining two very different styles of magic into a single evening's show. One was dextrous sleight of hand done "close in"—that is, on an intimate stage and with a minimum of props. The other was in mounting bold, large-scale stage illusions. Even in the simplest settings, Herrmann could always dazzle audiences. Writer-magician Walter Gibson states,

Herrmann the Great changed the performance of magic by combining intimate sleights of hand, such as the rabbit-in-the-hat trick (left), with large-scale illusions using props as immense as elephants (above).

"His austere air . . . gave him a distinguished appearance that enabled him to turn mere tricks into seeming miracles."[4]

Kellar

Harry Kellar (1849–1922) was the first major magician born in America. Ironically, Kellar was wildly popular in other parts of the world, a genuine rival to his near-contemporary Herrmann the Great, but had to spend most of his life abroad before he found success in his native land. Milbourne Christopher notes, "Harry Kellar performed on five continents before he was accepted as the virtual king of American magic."[5]

Kellar's importance and influence lay partly in his performance techniques, which brought a dash of straightforward and robust American style to a profession dominated by European performers. One aspect of this style was Kellar's emphasis on carefully planned presentations of large, showy acts. One of his most famous illusions was the "Levitation of Princess Karnac," in which a girl in Hindu costume was "hypnotized" and placed on a couch, then apparently levitated slowly six feet into the air. Many other illusionists had performed levitation tricks, but Kellar's was by far the most spectacular.

Another lasting influence was Kellar's personal stage manner, which had typically American characteristics. The brawny, bald Kellar did not adopt the distant, "devilish" appearance that Herrmann and other European magicians had made into the standard for conjurors. Instead, he employed a straightforward, bemused expression and a whimsical stage manner that immediately engaged audiences with its open friendliness. Walter Gibson writes that Kellar was "the cryptic, kindly, bald-headed gentleman who looked as though he wouldn't deceive his audience for the world, and then proceeded to do exactly that."[6]

Harry Houdini

Harry Houdini (1874–1926) was, without a doubt, the most famous magician who ever lived. Houdini was a household name during his lifetime, and no one since has filled his shoes. Even seventy-odd years after his death, his name is instantly recognizable and is synonymous with mystery, illusion, and suspense.

But Houdini was important for more than magic. In fact, he was not the most gifted of magicians. Adding to his lasting fame were two other factors: a flair for self-promotion, which ensured he was always in the headlines, and a strange and wonderful genius for escaping from seemingly foolproof restraints.

Houdini's tremendous fame stemmed from his ability to perform seemingly impossible escapes coupled with his extraordinary skills of self-promotion.

Houdini could escape from anything. Ropes, handcuffs, leg irons, sealed sacks, locked trunks, stocks and pillories, coffins, strait-jackets, prison cells, iron boilers that had been riveted shut, packing cases that had been nailed shut and thrown into rivers, water-filled glass cases in which he was hung upside down and shackled . . . nothing could hold Houdini.

During World War II, Jasper Maskelyne's ingenious illusions transformed military tanks into ordinary trucks and concealed whole armies by creating fake ones.

Today, the Houdini legend is further kept alive by the eerie coincidence of his death, which fell on Halloween, and by the persistent rumor that he hoped to contact the living from beyond the grave. Houdini continues to fascinate the world; as biographer Ruth Brandon notes, "He mystifies us to the end and beyond."[7]

Jasper Maskelyne

Jasper Maskelyne (1902–1973) was part of a dynasty of famous British illusionists that included his father, Nevil Maskelyne, and grandfather, John Nevil Maskelyne.

Jasper Maskelyne was already a well-respected magician when World War II broke out. However, his secret exploits during this bitter conflict, adventures that earned him the nickname of the War Magician, became his major contribution to the world of conjuring.

As an officer specializing in camouflage, Maskelyne used his skills in creating enormous illusions to fool the German enemy. Techniques of misdirection, disguise, and illusion, learned by Maskelyne as a boy from his father and grandfather, were put to use not on a theatrical stage but on the enormous testing grounds of North Africa, Europe, and the Mediterranean Sea.

These illusions included disguising spy ships to look like harmless yachts and making tanks look like harmless trucks. Maskelyne also created enormous fake armies while hiding real ones in the deserts of Egypt, where he "moved" the harbor of Alexandria. He even hid the entire Suez Canal from German bombers! According to writer David Fisher, Maskelyne's efforts constituted the ultimate challenge to a conjuror: to "pit the powers of magic against the most evil foe in history."[8]

David Copperfield

David Copperfield (b. 1956) is, by almost any reckoning, the world's most popular living illusionist. Thanks to his widely viewed television specials and live performances, it is probable that more people have seen Copperfield than any other magician in history.

His fame arises in large part through his ability to combine traditional magic with the awesome promotional powers of television. Like past masters such as Kellar and Houdini, Copperfield has a genius for self-promotion, as well as for mounting crowd-pleasing shows, creating a flashy stage persona, and using state-of-the-art performance techniques.

His tremendous popularity has brought Copperfield great fortune; he is one of the wealthiest entertainers in the world. It has also brought him notoriety, including keen public interest in his long-running romance with German supermodel Claudia Schiffer.

Many other contemporary magicians also bring aspects of traditional magic into present times. Among the most prominent of these are James Randi (the Amazing Randi), Harry Blackstone Jr., and the duo of Siegfried and Roy. No one, however, has done it on a larger scale, more flamboyantly, or more successfully than David Copperfield.

Penn and Teller

Penn Jillette (b. 1955) and Teller (b. 1948) are magic's number-one subversives.

Though they are often called "the bad boys of magic," the duo claims to prefer the phrase "professional ripoff artistes." They describe their performance as "a magic show for people who hate magic." Their act is so difficult to describe that when they were awarded an Obie (the prestigious off-Broadway theater equivalent to the Tony Award), the honor was officially given to them for "whatever it is they do."[9]

Penn and Teller combine aspects of genuine magic with a dazzling mix of ironic showmanship, outrageous black humor, and carnival-style antics. Onstage they present a dramatic study in contrasts: Penn, a compulsive motormouth, does little but talk, while Teller, who is generally acknowledged as one of the best sleight-of-hand artists alive, never says a word.

An important part of Penn and Teller's performance lies in their insistence on guiding audiences to understand and share in the deeper meanings behind what they do. They describe what is happening, showing exactly how a trick is done, and still amaze their audiences. This attitude gives their act a thought-provoking spin. At the end of a typical show, Penn will sit at the edge of the stage, eating fire, and tell the audience, "The question we want you to ask yourself is not *how* we do these tricks, but *why* we do them." [10]

Taken together, all of these performers exemplify the history of modern magic, from its birth in the 1800s, through its rise in the so-called golden age of magic in the late nineteenth and early twentieth centuries, and on to its present state, in which millions of people can be amazed and delighted by a single televised performance.

CHAPTER 1

Harnessing the Occult . . . Or Pretending To

Magic has been part of all human societies for thousands of years and in every corner of the world. Belief in magic is far older than science and more widespread than any single religion.

The use of specific magical spells, potions, and practices varied widely. Maori tribesmen in New Zealand, for instance, believed that they could improve a newly built canoe by reciting a chant that spoke of a bird on the wing, the lightness of a seagull floating on the water, and types of woods noted for their buoyancy. Members of the central African Azande tribe believed that rubbing the stem of bananas with a crocodile tooth would make them grow.

In Europe, the spell of magic was equally strong. Even the most powerful leaders were captivated by the abilities of their sorcerers. Greek and Roman emperors, for instance, believed that their magicians could tell the future by occult means such as reading bird entrails.

European magicians of the Middle Ages were often associated with the practice of alchemy. Alchemists were scientist-sorcerers who experimented with ways to turn ordinary base metals into gold. They also searched for the philosopher's stone, a mythical substance that they believed contained a universal spirit.

The so-called black arts—magic used for evil—included witchcraft, Satanic worship, sorcery (the use of spells), and necromancy (the calling up of the dead for consultation and prediction). Black magic was widely banned and feared, and its practice was punishable by death. Early Christians were so convinced that magicians were in league with the Devil that they created such practices as exorcism to destroy them.

Roger Bacon and Scientific Principles

During the Middle Ages, amazing phenomena that we now understand as scientific breakthroughs were often regarded as some form of sorcery. Early travelers to China, such as Marco Polo, for

Medieval scientist-sorcerers known as alchemists experimented with ways to transform common metals into gold and searched for the mysterious philosopher's stone.

instance, reported seeing cloth that would not burn (probably a form of asbestos) and witnessing the arrival of the sun at night (the result of burning gunpowder).

Perhaps the first great magician of Western society was Roger Bacon. Bacon, a Franciscan friar born in England about 1214, was also a scientist and alchemist. (There are many famous names connected with magic in past times. Merlin, the legendary sorcerer of King Arthur's court, is possibly better known than Bacon; however, there is no proof that Merlin really existed.)

Bacon devoted his life to the combined study of science, philosophy, and magic. He was intimately familiar with many illusions that could be performed through the use of scientific principles. Bacon was able to achieve wonders such as apparently producing music from invisible musicians upon a visit from King Henry III. He also seemingly created lightning and thunder on command and raised the ghosts of such legendary figures as Hercules.

Some of Bacon's tricks used principles of optics and physics still employed by stage magicians today. One of his journal entries, for example, essentially describes sleight of hand, ventriloquism, and other techniques: "There are men who create illusions by the rapidity of their hands' movements, by the assumption of various voices, by ingenious apparatus or by means of confederates so that they show to men wonderful things which do not exist."[11]

The use of basic physical and mechanical properties continues, remarkably unchanged, into the present day. The same principles of the natural world that Bacon used are used by today's conjurors. As a more recent British magician, Jasper Maskelyne, noted in his memoirs, "Modern magic, as I and others employ it in the theatre, is largely a matter of applied mechanics."[12]

Early Conjuring as Entertainment

Conjuring as entertainment, rather than as part of mystical or scientific research, has been part of life at least since the beginning of recorded histories. Most existing accounts about early conjurors come from the Middle Ages.

Typically, the most skilled of these conjurors served as entertainers for royalty. Those who were less skilled plied their trade on the streets or in markets, gathering contributions from passersby.

Popular tricks of the time included restoring an apparently severed piece of string and seeming to thrust knives into one's body. Perhaps the most widespread illusion performed by early conjurors, however, was the "Cup and Balls." The trick was a staple of conjurors in Egypt, China, and India, as well as in Europe.

Still a popular trick today, the Cup and Balls illusion uses three inverted cups to hide and manipulate a small ball or pebble. While the magician skillfully misdirects the audience's attention and manipulates a hidden ball, the visible ball seems to jump magically from one cup to another. It was so common and widespread that the Greek and Roman words for *conjuror* translate literally as "he who deals with pebbles."

In medieval times, European magicians were often itinerant; that is, they traveled widely and had no permanent homes. Their equipment was therefore limited to what they could carry easily on their backs, and they developed a wide range of tricks that could be performed with small objects—or, better yet, with borrowed objects such as fruit, chickens, hats, or handkerchiefs. (The more prosperous magicians could afford more equipment, which was carried on a horse or donkey.)

Itinerant conjurors often developed regular routes from city to city, and towns often designated specific streets along which magicians could ply their trade. Conjurors often joined up with other performers, such as acrobats or musicians, to provide more elaborate shows. Sometimes these shows were given in rented store-houses or barns, providing a larger venue (and more money) than the street could provide.

The advent of the printed playing card, which was easily obtained and carried, ushered in an enormously varied and still-popular staple of the magician's repertoire: the card trick. Such small-scale apparatus helped early conjurors refine their acts until

A medieval magician awes his audience using the centuries-old "Cup and Balls" trick.

they were, in the words of magic historian Ricky Jay, "the embodiment of what a magician should be—not a performer who requires a fully equipped stage, elaborate apparatus, elephants, or handcuffs to accomplish his mysteries, but one who can stand a few inches from you and with a borrowed coin, a lemon, a knife, a tumbler, or a pack of cards convince you he performs miracles." [13]

With his wicked leer and a common deck of cards, magician and magic historian Ricky Jay appears to perform the impossible.

Early Magic Books and Words

The earliest existing book to describe magic tricks is *The Discoverie of Witchcraft*, published in 1584 and written by Reginald Scot. Scot was not a magician himself; he wrote the book to convince the pubic that street performances contained only illusion, not genuine sorcery.

Other early books were *The Art of Jugling, or Legerdemain* (1614) and *Hocus Pocus Junior* (1634). Both contain clear descriptions of the secrets behind various illusions. Both books were written anonymously, probably because their authors feared the public might think that they had connections with much-feared witchcraft.

These early books reveal that certain secrets still used today, such as boxes with false bottoms, were in common use even hundreds of years ago. Likewise, several words and phrases still used by modern illusionists remain from these and even earlier times.

The word *magic* itself derives from a Greek version of the word *magi*, the occult priests of ancient Persia. *Abracadabra* dates back at least as far as the third century A.D. Some sources say it is related to the mystical Greek word *abraxas*, which translates literally to the number 365, said to be the number of orders of spirits emanating from the supreme being. Other sources conjecture that it is derived from the initials of the Hebrew words for the Holy Spirit.

Records exist from the year A.D. 208 in which a doctor on a Roman expedition to Britain recommends using the word *abracadabra* in a cure for fever. On a piece of paper hung around the patient's neck, the magical word was to be written in the form of a triangle:

```
ABRACADABRA
ABRACADABR
ABRACADAB
ABRACADA
ABRACAD
ABRACA
ABRAC
ABRA
ABR
AB
A
```

According to the doctor's notes, the fever would shrink, just as the word did, in nine days. Afterward, the paper was to be thrown over the patient's shoulder into a stream running eastward. The cure would then be complete.

The term *hocus pocus* is of somewhat more recent vintage. It was apparently invented by a street magician and theatrical performer whose real name is lost but who called himself Hocus Pocus. The name inspired many imitators in later years who gave themselves similar names, such as Hocus Pocus Junior and Master Hocus Pocus. In fact, the word *hoax* is thought to be derived from *hocus*.

One of the first references to the original Hocus Pocus appeared in 1656, when a writer named John Ady noted, "I will speake on one man . . . who called himself, The Kings Majesties most excellent Hocus Pocus, and so was called because that at the playing of every trick, he used to say, *Hocus Pocus, tontus talontus, vade celeriter jubio*, a dark composure of words, to blinde the eyes of the beholders, to master his trick pass the more currantly without discovery." [14]

"Doctors" and "Professors"

In the eighteenth and nineteenth centuries, as scientific knowledge began to dominate popular thought, magicians began asserting their great knowledge in these principles. Gradually, the general public lost the notion that conjurors could perform genuinely magical spells.

Performers of this period often used such titles as "Professor" or "Doctor" to assert their superior scientific knowledge. Often, they traveled the countryside in wagons that doubled as living quarters and stages, selling medicines and books that claimed to impart scientific secrets.

They promoted their legitimacy in other ways as well, not always successfully. Conjurors often advertised themselves in newspapers and on the street in posters, as with other forms of theatrical entertainment. Typical was one magician's claim to "exhibit the art of Legerdemain in a most superior style."[15]

Prominent magicians of the eighteenth and nineteenth centuries, such as Pinchbeck, Kalterfelto, and Bosco, could amass great fortunes and entertain before royalty. Nonetheless, magicians (and stage performers in general) were overall considered somewhat low class; theatrical performers were not yet the celebrated personages they would later become.

Still, they gradually became more accepted, and the art of stage magic progressed rapidly as mechanical innovations and performance techniques became more refined. The increased use of large-scale magical apparatus, such as mechanical automata, and the increasingly elaborate nature of certain performances, such as "thought transference" to an assistant, required more permanent settings. As a result, conjurors appeared more and more often on stage in semipermanent theaters rather than on the street.

Typically, these magicians wore ostentatious, flowing mock-Oriental costumes onstage. They cluttered their stages with

Using large-scale magical apparatus, a ghostly image is projected onto a stage. The props needed for such illusions required magicians to perform in more permanent locations.

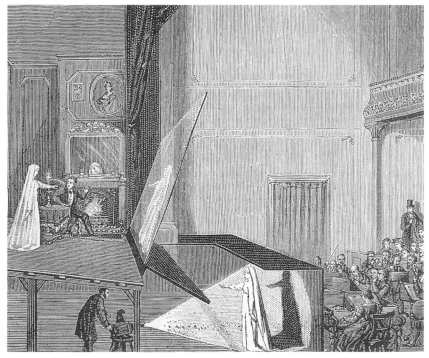

enormous amounts of equipment, although this clutter was mainly for show; only a few pieces would be used during any given performance.

The Flow of Knowledge

Throughout the centuries, magicians have fiercely guarded the secrets behind their most impressive illusions. As magician and writer Milbourne Christopher notes, "Once the secrets are known, the magician becomes a mere manipulator, an actor in a suspense drama which has little impact because the audience knows the ending in advance. Magicians guard their secrets to insure pleasure and surprise for audiences of the future." [16]

Despite this secrecy, the flow of magical knowledge down through the centuries has been extensive and in constant flux. One reason is simply that the principles of physics have not changed. Jim Steinmeyer, a designer of magical apparatus who works with David Copperfield, says, "The principles of magic are not new developments in physics. They are subtle, simple mechanics that aren't revolutionary in any way. The fact is, magicians [who hoard their secrets] are guarding an empty safe; it's valuable only as long as it's guarded." [17]

Furthermore, magicians have "borrowed" tricks from each other for generations. Many authorities claim that there have been precious few genuinely new magic tricks since Victorian times. Sometimes magicians legitimately purchase tricks from one another; sometimes they create significantly different variations; others use more blatant "borrowings." For instance, the most famous of modern magicians' tricks—sawing a person in half—was invented in 1921 by conjuror P. T. Selbit (whose real name was Percy T. Tibbles). It has been used in various forms, rarely with acknowledgment, ever since.

Even Penn and Teller, whose careers are based in part on undermining traditional magic shows, freely admit that aspects of their work are "borrowed" from illusions that have been in use for years. Penn wryly comments, "We . . . have, I think as much as anyone, drawn on a broad view of show business. I mean, we still have images in our show that were old at the time Houdini stole them." [18]

By the 1800s, magicians had brought their art from its humble beginnings, when it was steeped in superstitious belief and confined largely to tribal gatherings or the street, to a more refined position on the performance stage. Magic historian Walter Gibson notes, "By the early 1840s, magic had gradually but success-

Since it was first invented in 1921, the illusion of sawing a person in half has been "borrowed" and incorporated into the acts of countless magicians.

fully emerged from the clutches of traveling mountebanks and showmen who worked their hanky-panky in the booths of outdoor fairs." [19]

This period marked the beginning of modern magic. Among the most celebrated names of this era, performers who flourished in the mid-1800s, were Frikell, Hofzinser, and John Henry Anderson. The most gifted of these, the man generally considered to be "the Father of Modern Magic," was Robert-Houdin.

CHAPTER 2

Robert-Houdin: The Father of Modern Magic

Robert-Houdin was born Jean Eugene Robert in the small town of Blois, France, in 1805.

As a boy, Jean Eugene was interested in following in the footsteps of his father, a watchmaker. The elder Robert, however, hoped his son would become a lawyer. Jean Eugene obediently attended boarding school, which he hated, until he was old enough for a law apprenticeship. In his memoirs, he writes, "I can safely state that, though I was not averse to study, the happiest day I spent [in boarding-school] was that on which I left it for good." [20]

At the age of eighteen, Robert was appriced to a local lawyer. His primary job, copying legal documents by hand, took advantage of his excellent penmanship. The young man's heart was not in the study of law, however, and every morning, before work, he would slip into his father's workshop to make clockwork machines.

One such machine was a small box whose top showed an outdoor scene. Pressing a button caused a tiny mechanical rabbit to run across the landscape, followed by a hunter and his dog. When the hunter fired, the device made a "shooting" noise and the rabbit disappeared into a thicket.

Despite the cleverness and skill shown in the creation of these complex mechanisms, Robert's father still insisted his son pursue legal training. Robert became a senior law clerk, but he still spent all his spare time and energy creating small mechanical toys. He built a number of devices, such as miniscule birdbaths with tiny pumps to fill them, for a large cage of canaries the lawyer kept in his office. Robert later remarked, "The pleasure I felt in carrying out these small schemes soon made me forget I was in a lawyer's office for any other purpose than to be at the beck and call of canaries." [21]

Exposure to Magic

Eventually, Robert's father, seeing the young man's persistent interest, bowed to the inevitable and agreed that his son could abandon the law and take up the family trade. Soon, however, a new enthusiasm would come his way.

The young man's first exposure to magic, a street performer named Dr. Carlosbach, had been a disappointment; the "doctor" had sold the eager Robert a booklet that allegedly explained his tricks; but the book only described what they were, not how they were done.

A more enlightening volume came his way by accident. One evening, while still his father's apprentice, Robert went to a bookseller's shop to purchase a two-volume work entitled *Treatise on Clockmaking*. A distracted

A rare 1848 drawing of Robert-Houdin, the magician whose love of automata and obsession with magic would win him much acclaim.

shopkeeper gave him the wrong books, and the young man discovered he had instead a set of books on magic tricks called *Scientific Amusements*. The accident of fate, the magician later asserted, was a life-changing circumstance; the resemblance of the "wrong" books to the "right" ones and the haste of the bookseller, he wrote, were "the commonplace causes of the most important event in my life." [22]

Intrigued by the magic books, he began to learn their secrets. The dexterity he already possessed as a clockmaker served him well with sleight-of-hand tricks. He also paid a local performer to teach him juggling, which he practiced while reading.

Apprentice or Not?

According to his memoirs, Robert served an apprenticeship to a traveling magician named Torrini. Torrini, we are told, traveled in a wagon that could expand like a telescope to twice its regular length and serve as a compact theater. He also exhibited a number of automata (clockwork mechanisms that performed on their own), such as a jack-in-the-box that jumped from its box and danced before returning.

Robert allegedly spent several years with Torrini before he returned to his hometown, where he went to work in a clock shop. However, there is no evidence that Torrini really existed, and some scholars of magic suspect he was invented by Robert-Houdin to make his memoirs more thrilling.

Automata and Magic

Robert soon became bored with the routine work in the clock shop. He spent much of his time with an amateur theater troupe, where he met and in 1830 married a seventeen-year-old named Josèphe Houdin. Adding his father-in-law's name to his own, the young clockmaker became Jean Eugene Robert-Houdin.

Josèphe's father was a native of Blois and a skilled watchmaker who had moved to Paris to be in the wholesale clock and clock-parts business. With his father-in-law's encouragement, Robert-Houdin also moved to Paris and opened his own shop, repairing and building watches. On the side, he also created his own clever automata. Among these was an "alarm light" clock that not only sounded at the desired time but produced a lighted candle. He also built such mechanical toys as a windup magician, a dancer on a tightrope, and realistic singing birds.

Tragically, Josèphe died in 1843 and Robert-Houdin was left to care for their three small children. His business and personal life went into a decline for a brief period. However, his fortunes improved when he remarried in 1844 to Marguerite Bracconier.

Soon after, encouraged by his new wife, he began to enter his automata in exhibitions. One of these figures, a tiny man who wrote poetry and drew figures, caught the interest of Louis-Philippe, the king of France, and was later bought by the great American showman P. T. Barnum. Barnum, in his memoirs, wrote with a characteristic flourish that the Frenchman was "not only a prestidigitateur and legerdemain [trick] performer, but a mechanician of absolute genius." [23]

At the same time that he was creating his automata, Robert-Houdin maintained his interest in magic. He bought several items of magical apparatus. He also began to design and make automata that specifically involved aspects of magic, such as a "mysterious clock" with a transparent dial and stand that seemed to operate without any mechanism.

He also attended every show possible of magicians performing in Paris. He was particularly taken with a well-known magician and ventriloquist, Louis Comte, of whom he wrote in his *Memoirs*, "These performances of Comte . . . inflamed my imagination; I dreamed only of theatres, conjuring, mechanisms, automata, etc.; I was impatient to . . . make myself a name in the marvellous art." [24]

A New Career

As his success with the automata continued and his obsession with magic grew, Robert-Houdin began planning a new career for himself. This new direction included creating his own theater. With money borrowed from a wealthy friend, he rented an upstairs room in a suitable building, then hired an architect and builders to transform it into a small performance hall.

After twenty years of studying magic, building his own automata, and closely observing other magicians, the budding performer had clear ideas about what he wanted for his own show.

This mechanical chess-playing game, designed by Robert-Houdin, showcases his skill in producing complex automata.

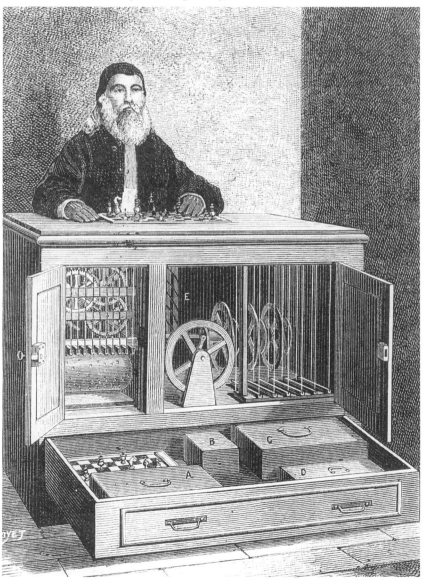

First of all, he wanted to put to work his idea that a magician's primary role was to provide convincing illusions in a theater, but in as natural a way as possible. This theatrical element, he felt, was an essential part of a successful magic show. A good magician, Robert-Houdin wrote, "is but an actor playing the part of a magician." [25]

One of Robert-Houdin's novel ideas was to build an entire evening's show around his automata, with other conjuring provided along with them to create an entire evening's entertainment. For many years, magicians had used a crude clockwork figure or two in their acts, but Robert-Houdin's plan—to use them as the main attraction in a performance—was an original and exciting idea.

Perhaps his most revolutionary idea, however, concerned his physical surroundings and appearance. His plan was to keep things simple; this was in sharp contrast to other magicians of the day, who generally tried to use as many imposing props and costumes as possible. Robert-Houdin insisted on clothing himself only in regular evening attire and on creating a simple stage with little clutter. Except for a few special illusions, he also did away with the use of assistants. Others, notably Frikell, had earlier advocated such simplicity, but Robert-Houdin's popularity and influence on future conjurors was great.

He felt that this simplicity would make his performances all the more mysterious to his audience. He also felt that it would focus attention on his own dexterity. He wrote, "I intended to have an elegant and simple stage, unencumbered by all the paraphernalia of the ordinary conjuror, which looks more like a toyshop than a serious performance. . . . I have always regarded such trickery [as assistants] as unworthy a real artist, as it raises doubts as to his skill." [26]

"Des Soirees Fantastiques"

In July 1845, Robert-Houdin's show, "Des Soirees Fantastiques," opened. (A soiree is an evening party.) His first appearances were disasters: he was nervous and spoke quickly and in a monotone. Few people came to see him.

As his confidence grew, however, his performances became better. He did sleight of hand with cards and other objects, such as "the surprising pocket-handkerchief." Borrowing a handkerchief from a spectator, he produced from it a variety of items, such as plums, feathers, and an entire basket of flowers.

The centerpiece of each performance, however, was his array of automata. One of the most famous was the "Orange Tree," which

Robert-Houdin and his young assistant amaze their audience by presenting the famous flowering "Orange Tree" act.

bloomed as if by magic with blossoms that transformed into oranges. He then tossed the fruit into the audience, who were astonished to discover that the fruit was quite real. The final touch of the Orange Tree act came when two mechanical butterflies fluttered over the tree.

Another famous automaton was the "Pastry Cook." A miniature chef appeared in the doorway of a pastry shop that was about the size of a child's dollhouse. At the spectators' requests, the little chef dashed into the shop and brought forth whatever cakes, buns, or other pastries had been called for. (The magician's son, Emile, hidden inside the "shop," filled the pastry cook's arms with the requested items.)

In his controversial variation of the "Ethereal Suspension" trick, Robert-Houdin appears to levitate his son.

Once the magician had sufficient confidence to be an expert performer, audiences began flocking to his theater. The magician soon added more amazing illusions. One was a "Second Sight" act performed with his son, who was able to identify objects despite being securely blindfolded. Another involved the newly discovered powers of electromagnetism; Robert-Houdin demonstrated weights, which he could lift easily but could not be budged by even the strongest audience member. (They were, of course, held in place at the touch of a switch.)

Still another famous trick was "Ethereal Suspension," during which the magician balanced himself on a delicate cane, apparently in defiance of gravity. In a variation, Robert-Houdin caused his son to seemingly float in the air; this trick aroused much passion among some spectators, who argued that the magician was guilty of child abuse.

Retirement

Robert-Houdin continued to perform regularly in his home theater for many years. He also appeared successfully in other parts of Europe, including several royal appearances before the queen of Belgium and England's Queen Victoria. Within a few years, he became the premier conjuror in the world.

The famous magician's career was illustrious but relatively short. In 1852, still at the height of his popularity, he decided to retire. He turned over his theater to a pupil, who was also his brother-in-law, and retreated to a country estate near Blois.

In retirement, Robert-Houdin spent much of his time working on clockworks powered by electricity. Robert-Houdin envisioned a time when electric clocks would be commonplace in daily life. In his memoirs, published when electricity was still a dangerous and unpredictable novelty, he wrote, "I already dream of the day when the electric wires, issuing from a single regulator, will radiate through the whole of France, and bear the precise time to the largest towns and the most modest villages." [27]

Besides electric clocks, Robert-Houdin's retirement mansion was outfitted with many other ingenious and then-novel devices, including an electrical fire alarm, a burglar alarm system, a swinging kitchen door that wound up a dinner bell as servants passed in and out, and a clock-operated system to automatically feed his horses in their stables.

One of the magician's most spectacular stunts actually took place after his retirement. On behalf of his country's government, he helped quell a serious rebellion overseas.

Against the Marabouts

In 1856, there was unrest in the French colony of Algeria. A group of Arab holy men, called marabouts, were inciting Algerians to attack French Foreign Legion troops stationed there. One method the marabouts used to arouse the populace was to convince them that they, the marabouts, had supernatural powers.

The French government thought that the best way to counter the holy men was to prove that their magic was fake. To this end, Robert-Houdin was invited to North Africa. The French magician decided it would be better not to expose the marabouts as fakes, but to convince the Algerians that his magic was superior.

In a series of performances, he seemingly created miracles. He used electromagnetism to prevent the strongest man in the audience from lifting an iron weight. He produced hot coffee from an apparently empty jug.

Robert-Houdin used his master showmanship, as illustrated here, to quell an Algerian rebellion.

He also invited an Arab from the audience to mark a lead bullet, which the magician loaded into a gun barrel. He then held an apple over his heart and invited the Arab to fire at it. As the Arab fired, Robert-Houdin staggered and then straightened, smiling. Opening the apple with a knife, he uncovered the bullet the Arab had marked. When challenged to repeat this feat in the open air, rather than in a theater, Robert-Houdin bettered himself by catching the bullet in his teeth.

This was clearly superior magic. Many of the dumbfounded spectators fell to the ground and began praying. Robert-Houdin's performances convinced the Algerians that they could not expect protection from French bullets, and the revolt fizzled.

Doubt

Some scholars of magic have questioned Robert-Houdin's true role in the history of the field. They claim that he simply "borrowed" ideas from others. The most famous magician of all, Harry Houdini, named himself after his hero Robert-Houdin, whose memoirs had inspired Houdini to become a magician in the first place. In his later years, however, for reasons that are not entirely clear, Houdini turned against his former idol and wrote a book denouncing him as a fraud and "the prince of pilferers."[28]

It is true that Robert-Houdin did not invent the idea of using mechanical figures; hundreds of magicians had demonstrated automata before his time. However, Robert-Houdin's mechanical marvels were far more complex and mystifying than any automata the world had yet seen. Claims that he stole illusions from other magicians of the time, such as the Scotsman John Henry Anderson, may well be true.

However, this "borrowing" was—and is—nothing new in the world of magic. Furthermore, even if he is guilty of such charges, there is no denying that Robert-Houdin was an important innovator in many lasting ways.

His insistence on a simplified stage, and on an elegant and refined performance manner and costume, set the standard for virtually every illusionist who followed him. These and other innovations expanded the frontiers of magic for the generations of magicians who succeeded him and ushered in the golden age of magic.

In 1871, at the age of sixty-five, the great magician died of pneumonia at his home near Blois.

CHAPTER 3

Herrmann the Great: The Devilish Magician

Like many famous magicians, Alexander Herrmann—known professionally as Herrmann the Great—was exposed to conjuring at an early age. Born in Paris in 1843, he was the son of a prosperous German-born doctor, Samuel Herrmann, who had once been an amateur magician himself. Furthermore, Herrmann's older brother Carl was already a full-time magician.

Carl Herrmann, twenty-seven years older than Alexander, had studied medicine, but the pull of his father's hobby was stronger. Against his father's strong wishes, Carl became a professional illusionist. He found great success; by the age of thirty he was Robert-Houdin's only serious rival and, as one of Europe's top performers, could boast such royal fans as Franz Josef of Austria, Ludwig I of Bavaria, Dom Pedro V of Portugal, and Frederick VII of Denmark.

When his younger brother Alexander was only a boy (some sources say he was eight, others ten), Carl asked him to come to Vienna, the city Carl had made his base. He wanted Alexander to be his assistant.

At first their father was as vigorously opposed to this as he had been to Carl becoming a performer, but he eventually relented. Alexander joined Carl in Austria for a period of intense study and apprenticeship to Carl. Alexander's stage debut was an auspicious one: performing in St. Petersburg before Czar Nicholas I of Russia.

Going Solo and Teaming Up

Alexander lived with Carl in Vienna, studying and serving as an apprentice, until he was fifteen. At that age he decided that he had acquired enough knowledge to become a solo performer. Displaying the bravado that would typify the rest of his life, he traveled to Madrid, Spain, and announced publicly that he was the best magician in the world. Somehow, the unknown young performer arranged a performance, apparently successful, before Spain's Queen Isabella II.

After this remarkable show, perhaps the only solo debut before royalty in magic history, Alexander continued to tour Europe for another three years on his own. By then, his skills rivaled those of his brother.

There is, however, little evidence of jealousy between them at this point. In fact, they both expanded their horizons and began a joint tour of the United States in 1861. One of their performances during this tour included a special appearance for President Lincoln at the White House. Carl Herrmann gave Lincoln a deck of cards and asked him to shuffle them. In a reference to the Civil War, then raging, Lincoln passed the deck to his secretary of war, Simon Cameron, and wryly said, "This gentleman shuffles the cards for me at present." [29]

Unfortunately, the brothers' tour of America was cut short by the unrest of the war. They embarked instead on a highly successful tour of South and Central America. This was the first of their major tours, and over the next several decades they continued to tour both jointly and on their own. It was during these years that Alexander chose to become "Herrmann the Great" onstage.

Eventually, the brothers agreed to an informal arrangement by which Alexander would perform mainly in America, Carl mainly in Europe. In part, this was because Alexander loved touring America, but it was also because of Carl's financial circumstances. Carl retired in 1870, comfortably rich, but then lost nearly everything through bad investments and at age fifty-seven was forced to return to the stage. Out of respect for his elder brother, Alexander performed mainly in America so that they would not compete.

Born into a family fascinated by magic, Alexander Herrmann followed in his father's and brother's footsteps, choosing to become a magician.

Sleights

Both brothers were brilliant sleight-of-hand performers. Carl, in later years, spurned the use of elaborate magic apparatus almost entirely, preferring instead to concentrate on pure sleight of hand.

One of Carl's specialties was hurling playing cards or photos of himself with amazing accuracy into all parts of a theater. He also excelled at concealing objects around his tall, slender frame. First producing a multitude of objects such as watches and handkerchiefs, he would then ask members of the audience to search his person for more; after they were assured there was nothing else concealed, he would blithely reveal more.

Alexander was equally dextrous, and he often used intimate surroundings to his advantage while working close in. For instance, he would borrow a hat from an audience member, discover a rabbit in it, then pull the rabbit apart to make two rabbits, and make the two dissolve into one. He would make the rabbit disappear, then find it in the coat of an audience member.

Another of Alexander's famous sleights was the "Miser's Dream." In this act, he borrowed a top hat from an audience member, then caught in it silver dollars that seemed to fall from nowhere. Pouring the money first into a silver tray that he displayed to the audience, then into a paper bag, the magician wrapped the whole up and tossed it to the owner of the hat—who was astonished to find that the money had changed to a box of candy.

Alexander's stage performances differed from his brother's, however, because he added illusions to his show that grew bigger and more elaborate each season. By the 1890s, there were three and sometimes four such spectacular scenes in every evening's program of magic by Herrmann the Great.

Big Illusions

In one such large-scale illusion, Herrmann cut off his female assistant's head, carried it across the stage, and had a conversation with her before restoring the head to its proper place. He burned his assistant alive, then resurrected her out of a paper cocoon, dressed as a butterfly. Not content to have a single gun shot at him so he could catch the bullet, an illusion Robert-Houdin had perfected, he lined up five riflemen and caught all five bullets at once.

One of Herrmann the Great's most famous illusions was later perfected by Houdini. In it, Herrmann apparently walked through a solid brick wall.

First, assistants spread a wide rug onstage. A larger sheet of seamless muslin was laid over it. Each was examined by members of the audience, to ensure that there were no holes or tears. Then a high brick wall, mounted on rolling casters only inches from the floor, was placed over the center of the rug.

MONDAY, Aug. 21, 1876.

EVERY EVENING at 8, and WEDNESDAY AND SATURDAY AFTERNOONS at 2,

FOR THIS WEEK ONLY!

The world-renowned and unapproachable Prestidigitateur,

PROF. A. HERRMANN

—— IN A ——

NEW WORLD OF MAGIC AND LEGERDEMAIN!

PROGRAMME.
PART FIRST.

1. Flying Cards.
2. Wonderful Mind-Reading of Cards.
3. Magic Cigar Case.
4. All Nations in one Bottle.
5. Invisible Knots.
6. Mysterious Rabbit.
7. Arabian Trick.
8. Coffin Du Gran Mogul.

PART SECOND.

Exposure of the Wonderful Spiritual Seance!

PART THIRD.

1. Indian Foulard.
2. Enchanted Flowers.
3. Sympathetic Doves.
4. Solomon's Letter.
5. Flying Watches.
6. Four in One.
7. Comic Scenes.
8. Wonder of the Nineteenth Century.

An 1876 playbill announces the week-long engagement of "Professor A. Herrmann," whose tricks include "Flying Cards" and the "Mysterious Rabbit."

The members of the audience were stationed around the wall, their feet firmly on the edge of the rug. Screens were arranged to shield the magician from the audience. He would wave one hand at the audience above the screen and then, a few moments later, would wave again, this time on the other side of the brick wall.

There was no way he could have gone under the wall, because it was only a few inches off the ground, or around the sides, because they were blocked by audience members. By all appearances, he had simply melted through the wall.

Pranks and Promotions

Herrmann the Great enjoyed performing feats of impromptu off-stage magic. While walking down a street, he would pause to produce candy from the ears of children and present them with it. Dining at a friend's house, he would drink a glass of wine, throw the glass in the air to make it disappear, then later in the evening borrow a napkin from another guest and, from underneath the cloth, produce the wineglass. Introduced to President Ulysses S. Grant at the White House, Herrmann produced a handful of cigars from the president's beard. By a strange coincidence, they were Grant's favorite brand.

Sometimes, however, Herrmann's impromptu magic backfired. Once, while dining in an elegant hotel restaurant with Bill Nye, a popular humorist of the day, Herrmann looked under the lettuce on Nye's plate and uncovered a diamond ring. Herrmann casually remarked on how careless he was.

Nye outsmarted the magician, however, by remarking that he himself was always leaving little things like that lying around. The humorist promptly picked the ring up and gave it to a passing waitress. Herrmann had to ask for the hotel manager's intercession to retrieve his ring. It is not recorded what compensation the waitress received for having been the butt of this prank.

Herrmann was also a great believer in self-promotion. Once, in London, he walked up to two men on Regent's Street, a busy thoroughfare, and clumsily picked a handkerchief from one man's pocket, making sure two nearby policemen saw him. The officers accosted him, at which point the other man discovered his watch was missing.

The magician swore he had taken neither handkerchief nor watch and insisted on being searched. The policemen found neither object on Herrmann. The magician then asked the officers to look in their own pockets, and to their astonishment found both watch and handkerchief.

By now, the two men had recognized Herrmann and were laughing at the hoax, but the policemen were not amused. They took Herrmann to the nearest station and lectured him on disturbing the dignity of the police, which, of course, is exactly what the magician wanted, since the resulting publicity was in his favor.

Herrmann, like all good magicians, also had a knack for making mistakes look like deliberate acts. Once, he had an egg hidden under his vest for use in a later trick. While performing a card sleight early in the show, he "sprang" the deck, making it cascade from one hand to the other. His hand accidentally brushed his vest hard enough to loosen the egg, which fell and broke. Recovering quickly from this disaster, Herrmann smiled triumphantly at his audience and remarked, "Wonderful! An egg from a pack of cards!" [30]

At Home

Herrman's career included many appearances before world leaders. On one tour of Europe, he performed before Czar Alexander III of Russia. According to legend, the czar, a believer in the superiority of brute strength, tore a pack of playing cards in half with his hands and dared Herrmann to do better. The magician calmly put one half of the torn deck on top of the other and tore the whole thing in half again.

But Herrmann was most at home in the United States, so much so that he became a naturalized citizen. Life in America provided him with fame and fortune. He also gained a wife there—or on his way there, at least.

En route from England to the United States by ship in 1875, he met Adelaide Scarsez, a dancer who had been born in London to Belgian parents. She was on her way to be with her fiancé, but by journey's end she had changed her mind about the impending marriage. Instead, she became Herrmann's assistant and, later, his wife. Herrmann once mischievously remarked about this sudden switch, "I had reached right into her body and taken her heart just as I pick the pockets of people in my act. But this I have never given back to her and I never will!" [31]

During his long career, Herrmann the Great performed for numerous world leaders, including the infamous Russian czar Alexander III (pictured).

A measure of Herrmann the Great's status was that the couple's wedding ceremony was performed by the mayor of New York City. The mischievous Herrmann could not resist a prank during the ceremony: at one point, he reached into the mayor's abundant beard and pulled out a roll of dollar bills.

Between their frequent tours, the Herrmanns lived in a huge mansion in Whitestone, Long Island, near New York City. Herrmann kept an enormous yacht, the *Fra Diavolo*, ready to travel into New York Harbor to pick up friends who had sailed from Europe. In the days when travel by truck, bus, or plane was not yet possible, Herrmann also maintained a private rail car on a siding at the Whitestone station. This was the couple's home away from home while on tour, and was used in conjunction with two baggage cars for the considerable equipment required for his show.

At home, the couple lived a life of luxury and entertained the top performers and artists of the day. Writer and magician Walter Gibson comments that Herrmann's mansion "became a gathering place for the elite of the American theatrical world, who regarded Herrmann as one of their outstanding luminaries." [32]

Last Tours

Within a few years of coming out of retirement, Alexander's older brother Carl accumulated another fortune to replace the one he had lost. Carl remained one of the top entertainers in Europe, and on the occasion of his seventieth birthday received many birthday greetings from notable people. One was a wry note from Queen Marie Henrietta of Belgium, who had studied conjuring with him: "Do not be afraid; I have not divulged your secrets to anyone." [33]

The brothers made a final joint tour of Europe in the mid-1880s. Carl was still actively performing when he died in 1887 at the age of seventy-one.

Alexander also performed until his death in 1896. He died of a heart attack while on a train from his home to an engagement in Pennsylvania. Milbourne Christopher, noting the many heartfelt memorials accorded to Herrmann the Great from around the world, writes, "His obituaries were the most extensive ever published for a conjuror." [34]

Herrmann's legacy and lasting fame stem partly from his having virtually invented the familiar devilish look many magicians still embrace: tall, slender, and commanding, with magnetically charismatic eyes and a sharp goatee known as an imperial beard. Writer-magician T. A. Waters notes that Alexander's physical appearance "is still associated with a magician in the popular

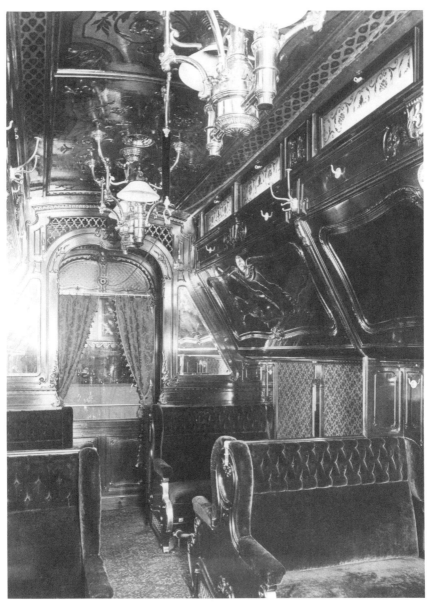

The Herrmanns had their own private rail car, which they used as their home away from home while on tour.

mind. . . . He created an image of the magician—not only in appearance, but also in style and manner—which continues to influence performers nearly a century after his death." [35]

Alexander's death roughly marked the midpoint of the era many historians of the field call the golden age of magic. In the years afterward, Carl's and Alexander's nephew Leon Herrmann

Herrmann the Great defined what a magician should look like; even today, many magicians, including Harry Blackstone Jr. (pictured), assume a devilish appearance.

toured America and Europe as a conjuror. Alexander's widow, Adelaide, also performed for many years after her husband's death, both with Leon and solo. Neither, however, had the skill or magnetic charisma of their predecessors. Rival magicians, notably Harry Kellar, gradually took over the two brothers' place at the top of the entertainment world.

CHAPTER 4

Kellar: The First Great American Magician

Harry Kellar, the first major magician to be born in the United States, started life as Heinrich Keller, the son of a German immigrant, in Erie, Pennsylvania, in 1849. Some sources give his first name as Harold. In either case, everyone knew him as Harry.

Even as a boy, Harry demonstrated a flair for the dramatic. Sometimes, on a dare, he would stand motionless on the railroad tracks as a train approached, jumping aside just moments before it passed by. According to legend, this penchant for dangerous experimentation was the reason the boy left his hometown at the age of ten.

From Explosions to Joining the Fakir

Harry, apprenticed at Dr. Squill's Drugstore, liked to play around with chemicals. One day, he created an explosive mix of sulfuric acid and soda, which blasted a hole in the drugstore's floor. The druggist, understandably, fired the boy. Rather than explain to his strict German father that he had lost his job, Harry hopped a freight train bound for Ohio.

In Cleveland, he found work at a dry-goods store and a newspaper, then caught another freight train to New York City. There, he sold papers and slept in the office of a hotel in exchange for helping a night porter clean up. Harry was then taken under the wing of a British-born clergyman, Robert Harcourt, who took him to the small upstate New York town of Canandaigua, offering to adopt him and pay for his education if he agreed to study for the ministry.

Harry saw his first magician when he and his benefactor visited a traveling show in the nearby town of Penn Yan. The magician called himself the Fakir of Ava, and his act included performing such wonders as producing coins from nowhere and changing paper shavings into various substances such as milk, sugar, and hot coffee. He also performed a stunt involving smashing a

Harry Kellar was the preeminent magician in the United States at the beginning of the twentieth century.

borrowed watch, loading the pieces into a widemouthed gun, and firing at a target, where the watch would miraculously appear, fully restored.

Kellar said later that this experience immediately created in him the urge to go on the stage, despite the handicaps of having short stubby fingers and a slight stutter. He bought books on magic and began studying them intently. He also resolved to leave his benefactor, Dr. Harcourt, whom he felt would never approve of his protégé pursuing an uncertain and low-class life on the stage.

Harry left Canandaigua and wandered again, ending up as a chore boy on a farm in Buffalo. One day, he saw in a local newspaper an ad announcing that the Fakir of Ava needed an assistant.

Offstage, the magician was an Englishman named Isaiah Harris Hughes, who had settled near Buffalo.

The boy ran the two miles to the magician's home and, according to legend, got the job because he was the only applicant who was not attacked by Hughes's dog. Walter Gibson writes, "Dozens of boys had already applied, but the little dog had snapped and snarled at all of them, until Hughes had decided that he would hire the first boy that the dog liked." [36]

From Assistant to Solo Act

The Fakir of Ava's assistant proved a capable helper, especially when improvisation was needed.

Once, before the shooting-the-watch trick, Harry forgot to hang a watch on the back of the fakir's target in preparation for its "miraculous" reappearance. As the gun went off, Harry thought fast: he grabbed an envelope and ran into the audience, shouting "Telegram for Major de Quincy Jones." With everyone's attention diverted, Harry was able to drop a spare watch in a spectator's pocket. Then he went onstage and whispered to the fakir. The magician then changed his act quickly, retrieving the watch with a "spirit bell" that correctly "told" which row and seat number the watch's "owner" was in.

At the age of sixteen, Harry decided he had learned enough from the fakir to try performing himself. He decided to call himself Kellar, changing the spelling of his name to avoid confusion with Heller, a well-known magician of the day.

Kellar's first solo shows were notably unsuccessful. He debuted in Dunkirk, Michigan, and played several other small towns. All the shows were flops, however, and he returned to the fakir's employ for two more years before trying again to establish a solo career.

This time he was more successful, although there were some close calls. At one point Kellar was cheated by a promoter in Indiana who skipped town with all the profits. When the local sheriff seized the magician's property in lieu of unpaid bills, Kellar fled by hopping a train with only the clothes on his back.

En route to Milwaukee, the young magician was thrown off the train in a small town and walked in the snow to Waukegan, Illinois. A sympathetic bartender there gave him a topcoat and a pair of overshoes. Kellar then talked the manager of a hall into letting him give two performances with no deposit, and convinced a printer to produce advertising handbills on credit. The bartender gave him two packs of playing cards and Kellar scrounged other items that served as impromptu magic equipment. The shows were successful, and Kellar was able to pay back his debts, reclaim his magic equipment, and buy a ticket out of Waukegan.

From the Davenports to South America

Kellar continued to tour the Midwest, but real success eluded him. Disheartened, he went to work in 1869 for the Davenport Brothers. The Davenports were the first successful stage mediums; that is, they were alleged spiritualist mediums who had adapted "psychic" séances into a popular performance act. In fact, all of their psychic phenomena were performed by means of tricks known to conjurors everywhere, such as secretly escaping from apparently solid bonds in order to ring bells or shake tambourines.

Kellar graduated from assistant to advance agent and then business manager for the brothers, then quit the troupe in 1873 to go solo again. This time, he teamed up with another former Davenport assistant, a "psychic reader" named William Fay. Together, they successfully toured Canada in the summer of 1873. This was the beginning of Kellar's penchant for extensive travel, which would last for most of his professional life.

By December, Kellar and Fay were in Havana, Cuba. When an interpreter demanded too much money, Kellar decided he would memorize his stage patter (the talk that accompanies an entertainer's routine) in Spanish. Within a few weeks, he later reported, his Spanish was "good enough to make people understand and bad enough to amuse them." [37]

Kellar worked closely with the Davenport Brothers (pictured), successful stage mediums who used common conjuring tricks.

Kellar and Fay continued southward, playing across Mexico despite primitive and uncertain travel conditions. In Mexico City, a newspaper announced that the pair performed their miracles with demonic assistance, and it warned people to stay away. Nonetheless, the duo made a lot of money—enough so that when traveling they prudently hid their gold coins in cans of sticky black paving material, tucked in among their magic equipment, as a deterrent against roving bandits.

By early 1875, Kellar and Fay had worked their way down the west coast of South America and were moving up the east side. They had many adventures along the way: In Montevideo, a rival magician challenged Kellar, saying he would tie the American up so securely that he could never get out. Kellar agreed, on the condition that the loser would donate the equivalent of two thousand dollars to charity. The Spanish magician tied him up, but Kellar was out in seconds. Farther along his route, in Rio, Kellar gained the first of many royal admirers, when Brazil's emperor Dom Pedro II became a big fan and saw the show several times.

Disaster and Recovery

Disaster struck when Kellar and Fay set out by ship for England in the summer of 1875. Their ship ran aground in the Bay of Biscay, and two crewmen drowned. The survivors were rescued by a French warship and taken ashore, but Kellar was able to save only a diamond ring. Lost were all his clothes, his magic equipment, and more than twenty thousand dollars in mementos, diamonds, and gold and silver coins.

Worse luck met the magician in London. He received word that his New York bank had failed, so he could receive no money from his account there. He was forced to sell his diamond ring to cover immediate expenses.

His discouraged partner, Fay, left to rejoin the Davenport Brothers, but Kellar remained for a time in London. Attending a performance at the Egyptian Hall, that city's center for magical performance, he saw a stunning new illusion by a fellow magician, Buatier de Kolta: a cage and canary that vanished into thin air. Kellar bought the trick from de Kolta for $750.

This illustrates a trait Kellar showed all his professional life: a tendency to use illusions invented by others, rather than create his own. Will Goldston, a noted magician and writer, wrote in the 1930s about Kellar:

> If he saw an illusion which appealed to him he would get it, if not by fair means, then by foul; although I will do him

Carriages crowd near the entrance of London's Egyptian Hall, a theater renowned for its magical performances.

justice by saying that he always first attempted to strike an honest bargain over such deals. If his preliminary overture failed, he would find out, either by bribery or close observation, how the trick was performed. Then, when a suitable period had elapsed, he would incorporate it in his own programme.[38]

Buying de Kolta's illusion nearly used up Kellar's resources, and he had to borrow money to get to New York. He managed to get thirty-five hundred dollars from the wreckage of his collapsed bank, enough to buy props to sustain a complete show. Then he sailed back to London, repaid the loan, and put together a troupe that included a pair of Hungarian brothers, one a fire-eater and the other a contortionist, who billed themselves as Ling Look and Yamadeva.

Kellar and his troupe then set off for a world tour: the West Indies, South America, the western part of the United States, Australia, Asia, Africa, and the Middle East. This was, by now, almost second nature for the magician. As Milbourne Christopher writes, "Harry Kellar was the great traveler of his day, as much at home in Calcutta, Capetown, or Rio de Janeiro as in New York or London."[39]

There were some rough spots along the way. The Australian Society for the Prevention of Cruelty to Animals, for instance, picketed Kellar's show, insisting that he killed a canary each time he made de Kolta's cage disappear. He proved them wrong by tying a silk thread around the bird's leg, then making it disappear and reappear with the thread intact.

In general, however, the tour was a resounding success and played before capacity audiences everywhere. Kellar entertained, among others, the sultan of Soerkarta in Indonesia, the maharajah of Johore in India, and the sultan of Zanzibar. Typical of audience reaction was this report from the Sydney (Australia) *Herald*: "The applause was deafening, and shouts of 'bravo' resounded from all parts of the house."[40]

More Globe-trotting

Back in London, Kellar, now twenty-nine, invested the princely sum of twenty thousand dollars in new equipment and headed back to New York. Unfortunately, Heller—the popular magician with the similar name—had recently died, and many critics and potential audience members thought Kellar, a newcomer to the New York stage, was trying to cash in on the similarity of names.

It did no good for Kellar to point out that he had long ago changed his name precisely to *avoid* confusion. Not even explanatory praise, such as this bit of doggerel from the *Asian*, a newspaper in Calcutta, India, did any good:

> For many a day
> We have heard people say
> That a wondrous magician was Heller.
> Change the H to a K
> And the E to an A
> And you have his superior in Kellar.[41]

The New York engagement was a failure, and Kellar once again had to borrow money to go elsewhere; in this case, to South America, where he had had such success before, followed by engagements in the United Kingdom that included one before Queen Victoria at Balmoral Castle, her summer retreat in Scotland. Then it was off for another round-the-world voyage, which took him to several Mediterranean countries and to South Africa and Asia.

By now Kellar had perfected his show, which relied heavily on his considerable powers to hold an audience's attention.

Milbourne Christopher writes, "Kellar used to say that once he had the audience's attention, an elephant could lumber across the stage behind him and no one would see it." [42]

Princess Karnac

Much of Kellar's lasting fame and influence stemmed from his performance techniques. These were what many observers call

An 1875 playbill for the popular magician Robert Heller. After Heller's death, many people accused Kellar of trying to capitalize on the similarity of their names.

OPERETTA HOUSE, WATERLOO PLACE.

FIRST ENTIRE CHANGE OF PROGRAMME,

TO-NIGHT, AND EVERY EVENING AT 8.

Illuminated Matinees every WEDNESDAY and SATURDAY at 3, specially recommended to Ladies, Children, Private Schools, and Suburban Residents.

FIFTH WEEK'S DIGNIFIED SUCCESS! GENUINE APPLAUSE!! LAUGHTER PREDOMINANT!!! MYSTERY TRIUMPHANT!!!!

EXTRAORDINARY AND SUSTAINED POPULARITY IN EDINBURGH OF

HELLER'S WONDERS

As Originated, Invented, and Performed only by

MR. ROBERT HELLER,

The Unrivalled American Entertainer, assisted by his Sister,

MISS HAIDEE HELLER,

And introduced with astounding success in England, America, California, Australia, New Zealand, India, Ceylon, China, and Java.

Fauteuils (2 front rows), 4s.; Reserved Carpeted Stalls (6 rows), 3s.; Front Area, 2s.; Area, 1s.; Gallery, 6d. Children and Schools Half-price, except Gallery. Places may be secured in advance at Messrs WOOD and Co.'s, Music Sellers, George Street.

That the Public may be satisfied of the Truth of every Announcement, Mr. Heller's Portfolio of Press Opinions and Travels can always be inspected on application.

SECOND MONSTRE PROGRAMME OF WONDERS, COMMENCING APRIL 26, 1875.

Part 1.—PRESTIDIGITATION and NECROMANCY.
1.—The Desicated Canaries.
2.—Fortunes and Misfortunes of a Handkerchief.
3.—The Witches' Pole.
4.—Ravel. (A French Clown.)
5.—A Curious Omelet.
6.—The Money Hunt.

Part 2.—MUSIC.
Mr. HELLER will perform three Brilliant Solos on a Magnificent Grand Pianoforte, by BLUTHNER, of Leipsic, specially selected by the eminent piano manufacturer, WADDINGTON, YORK, and purchased by W. J. BULLOCK, expressly for HELLER'S Wonders.
I.—MAZURKA, "JOSEPHINE."—*Heller.*   II.—CAPRICE, "Il Trovatore."—*Heller.*
III.—BALLAD, "AULD ROBIN GRAY," performed on the Orgue Melodique.—*Heller.*

Part 3.—MYSTERY.
The PHENOMENON of SUPERNATURAL VISION, as exemplified by

MISS HAIDEE HELLER,

Introducing the Marvellous SEALED PACKET MYSTERY for the first time in Scotland.

Part 4.—INSTRUCTIVE.
Mr. HELLER will conclude his Programme with a novel and interesting performance, entitled

PARLOR MAGIC.

W. J. BULLOCK, Responsible Manager.

characteristically American: dramatically straightforward and robust, unlike the highly refined European performers who dominated the profession.

Kellar's stage style also reflected typically American characteristics. The brawny, bald-headed Kellar disdained the "devilish" appearance Herrmann and other European magicians favored. Instead, he used to great effect a somewhat bemused expression and a mischievous, whimsical stage manner.

He also perfected using magic as a complete evening's entertainment, rather than simply one part of a show that might include musical interludes and other acts.

Kellar's large, lavish illusions were always carefully planned presentations. One of the most famous of these was his levitation of a person. This had been done previously in various forms by such famous magicians as Robert-Houdin (who had, in turn, adapted his illusion from one created by an Indian fakir). Never before, however, had it been done to such spectacular effect.

In Kellar's version, the "Levitation of Princess Karnac," a young woman in Hindu costume was apparently hypnotized and placed on a couch in the center of a fully lighted stage. Prompted by the magician, she then floated slowly up and remained suspended six feet in the air. The couch was removed and Kellar, standing on a short ladder, passed a solid hoop completely around the floating lady. A magic author of the day, John Northern Hilliard, wrote for Kellar's program a description that enthusiastically called it

> the most daring and bewildering illusion and by far the most difficult achievement Mr. Kellar ever attempted. [It] surpasses the fabled feats of the ancient Egyptian sorcerers, nor can anything more magical be found in the pages of the Thousand and One Nights, and it lends a resemblance to the miraculous tales of levitation that come out of India. . . . Its perfection represents fifteen years of patient research and abstruse study, and the expenditure of as many thousands of dollars. [A] veritable masterpiece of magic, the sensational marvel of the twentieth century and the crowning achievement of Mr. Kellar's long and brilliant career.[43]

His Own Hall

In 1884, after some dozen world tours, Kellar tried his luck once again in his homeland. This time, he fulfilled a long-held dream by opening his own theater: Masonic Hall in Philadelphia, which he renamed Kellar's Egyptian Hall. The venture proved successful, and many celebrities, including Mark Twain, saw one of the two hundred and sixty-seven performances Kellar mounted there.

By the end of this run, Kellar was firmly established as one of America's top performers. The 1886–87 season saw him back in New York City and touring the Midwest, breaking attendance records everywhere he went.

In 1887, while on tour in Michigan, Kellar married Eva Medley, whom he had met in her native Melbourne, Australia, when she was a teenage fan. Eva became a featured part of Kellar's act; blindfolded, she solved intricate math problems and performed other feats of mental magic. She was also the "victim" in such large-scale illusions as the "Divorce Machine," in which a woman sitting in a suspended chair disappeared as a shot was fired.

Kellar had succeeded in becoming one of the top magicians in America, but he was not the top. That honor still belonged to Alexander Herrmann. The two developed an intense rivalry for a

Writer Mark Twain was among the many celebrities who attended Kellar's performances at Philadelphia's Masonic Hall.

time, characterized by their advance men regularly pasting over each other's billboards. Not until Herrmann's death in 1896 did Kellar finally emerge preeminent.

With his success at last guaranteed, Kellar and his wife bought a comfortable home in Yonkers, a New York City suburb. In 1902, Kellar became the first dean (or president) of the Society of American Magicians (SAM), which was founded that year.

In 1904, the magician met Paul Valadon, a young German conjuror, and was impressed enough to invite him to become part of his troupe. Kellar was looking for a successor as he grew closer to retirement age. After several seasons of Valadon appearing on Kellar's bill, it appeared that the younger man was being groomed to take Kellar's place. However, Valadon's unpleasant personality proved his undoing. Magician and writer Will Goldston notes, "Valadon, although a very able conjuror, possessed a violent temper, and few people were able to bear his company for any length of time. . . . The older man could not see eye to eye with him on many matters, and quarrels were frequent."[44]

A Final Tour

By 1907, Kellar had dropped Valadon and another gifted magician, an American named Howard Thurston (1869–1936), became Kellar's heir apparent. Kellar's final tour costarred Thurston. At the last show of this tour, in May 1908 in Baltimore, Maryland, Kellar ended his forty-five years onstage by presenting Thurston with his treasured magic wand. Thurston went on to become the most popular magician in America for many years.

Kellar's retirement home was a mansion in Los Angeles. Unfortunately, two years after his retirement, his wife, Eva, who had been in ill health for some time, passed away. Kellar was then cared for by a niece and her husband. Milbourne Christopher notes that it was a comfortable retirement: "Despite setbacks through the years caused by shipwrecks, tropical fever, dishonest associates, and tremendous competition from rival theatrical attractions, Kellar had a comfortable fortune."[45]

Kellar was hardly idle in his retirement. Many famous magicians were his guests when they passed through Los Angeles, including his close friend Houdini, who had emerged as the most

Howard Thurston, with his elaborate stage productions, was Kellar's successor as the supreme magician in the United States.

55

popular magician in the world. He also spent much of his time tinkering in a workshop and performing impromptu shows in a miniature theater in his home.

Kellar's only major public appearance after retirement, however, was in 1917. Harry Houdini persuaded the aging master to appear at a benefit show in New York for the families of the first American casualties of World War I. After he had performed his act, Kellar tried to walk offstage, but Houdini stopped him. Doting members of SAM helped Kellar into a sedan chair. As they carried him off he was showered with roses and chrysanthemums, the orchestra played "Auld Lang Syne," and six thousand spectators gave him a standing ovation.

Harry Kellar died in 1922 in Los Angeles, of complications from influenza.

CHAPTER 5

Harry Houdini: King of Escapes

Houdini, the world's most famous man of mystery, loved to invent stories about himself. One tale he always insisted was true was that he was born Ehrich Weiss on April 6, 1876, in Appleton, Wisconsin. In fact, he was originally called Erik Weisz and was born on March 24, 1874, in Pest, Hungary, one of six children in a poor Jewish family.

Soon after Erik's birth, his father, a religious scholar, immigrated to America. He settled first in Appleton and then Milwaukee, where his wife and children later joined him. (The spelling of the family name, and of baby Erik's name, changed after the move.) Life in America was difficult, and the Weisses were always one step ahead of the bill collectors. By eight, Ehrich was selling newspapers and working as a bootblack to supplement the family income. He later wrote of this period, "Such hardships became our lot that the less said on the matter the better." [46]

Master magician Harry Houdini displays a complicated restraint used during one of his illustrious escapes.

Life in America

From an early age, Ehrich was interested in performing. According to his self-made legend, he began his career with a traveling circus at the age of nine. In fact, the "traveling circus" was a backyard affair, with "the

Prince of the Air" performing in homemade red stockings on a homemade trapeze.

Restless to see the world, Ehrich ran away from home at age twelve for about a year. In the meantime the Weisses relocated to New York City, though life was no easier there. About one of the many tiny flats they rented, Houdini commented, "We lived there, I mean starved there, several years." [47]

Ehrich the New Yorker held a variety of jobs, including department store messenger, assistant necktie cutter, and photographer's assistant. This last job he shared with his brother Theo; their boss was an amateur magician, and the boys apparently learned their first magic trick, vanishing a coin, from him. They both took to magic and began performing informally.

They also read everything they could find, including *The Memoirs of Robert-Houdin*. Ehrich became so obsessed with Robert-Houdin that a friend suggested he invent a stage name by adding an *i* to his idol's name. The other part of his stage name, Harry, was simply an Americanization of his nickname, Ehrie.

Bess

At seventeen, Houdini quit his job and became a full-time entertainer. His first professional appearances included street performances and brief tours of "dime museums," halls that offered variety shows for ten cents. Here he worked solo and with Theo, appearing alongside such acts as sword swallowers, fire eaters, comedians, and dancers. For their meager wages, the two performed as many as twenty shows a day, six days a week.

While performing at an amusement park, Houdini met Beatrice (Bess) Raymond, an aspiring singer and dancer. That Houdini was Jewish and Bess Catholic did not slow their blossoming romance. They married in 1894, and Bess immediately joined Houdini onstage. (Theo renamed himself Hardeen and started a solo career.)

Bess joked that she joined the act only to keep Houdini from looking at other women. In fact, she was a genuine boon; not only was she experienced onstage, but her small size made her ideal for the act's climactic stunt, a trunk-substitution trick called "Metamorphosis."

Houdini, so focused on work that he paid little attention to the details of daily life, relied heavily on Bess for the rest of his life. She washed his ears every day, because he never bothered to do it himself. Once, Bess packed him a week's worth of shirts when he was going on tour alone. When he got home, all but one of the shirts lay untouched, still in the order she'd packed them in.

The couple never had children, and (except for Hardeen) Houdini was not close to his brothers and sisters. Bess became his closest companion and his stalwart keeper. Biographer Ruth Brandon notes, "The two were rarely apart: Houdini would frequently write to her from another room in the same house." [48]

Escapes

Houdini's early shows emphasized traditional magic. In terms of sheer ability, he was not as gifted a conjuror as Kellar or other masters, and he was hampered by his short stature, a high-pitched

Married in 1894, Harry and Bess Houdini shared an intimate private life and a flamboyant stage act.

speaking voice, and the tough, ungrammatical speech he had learned on the streets of New York: "Ladies and gents, as youse can see I ain't got nothin' up my sleeve."[49]

However, Houdini's personal charisma and intensity made up for his shortcomings, and gradually his stage act became more polished. Then he hit upon the element that would make him famous: adding handcuff escapes to his show.

Handcuff escapes were not new; they had been performed since at least 1871, when a magician named Samri Baldwin had featured them in his act. Houdini's twist was to make them the centerpiece of his show . . . and to do them better.

Houdini studied various models of cuffs until he knew them inside out. He discovered that some opened when sharply rapped at a certain spot; others could be picked with a pin-size piece of metal.

He became so confident of his abilities that he began walking into police stations while on tour, offering a reward to anyone who could cuff him so thoroughly that he could not escape. He always won, and always in record time.

After several years of anonymity, the Houdinis' fortunes changed when Martin Beck, the head of a prestigious chain of theaters, suggested that Houdini drop the magic completely and fill his entire show with escape acts. The advice made Houdini a star; soon he headlined shows across the country. Never short on self-confidence, the escape artist began advertising himself with characteristic melodrama: "HARRY HOUDINI! The ONLY Recognized and Undisputed King of Handcuffs and Monarch of Leg Shackles."[50]

A Star

The Houdinis' fortunes really soared after they toured Europe and Russia. These years transformed Houdini from a minor figure in America into a major international celebrity.

The Houdinis arrived in London in 1900 with no bookings and enough money for only a week's room and board. But Houdini secured a brief engagement at a vaudeville house and was an immediate success, helped by such publicity stunts as an escape from handcuffs personally placed on him by the superintendent of Scotland Yard. Houdini's engagement stretched to six months, and he was soon earning twice his top salary in America.

A string of capacity engagements across Europe followed, attracting ecstatic crowds and lavish praise everywhere. Typical was this newspaper report of a show in Essen, Germany:

Not alone was the house sold out, but hundreds were turned away. Contrary to fire and police regulations, the aisles were packed and . . . chairs were placed on the stage to accommodate the public. Not even the fearful heat could keep away this sweltering mass of humanity and prevent it from giving Houdini an ovation. [51]

The couple returned to New York in 1905, and Houdini used his new wealth to purchase a twenty-six-room Manhattan home. Houdini called it the finest home any magician ever had, forgetting in his enthusiasm such palatial estates as Herrmann's Long Island mansion or Robert-Houdin's lavish château.

The house was roomy enough to contain Houdini, his mother, his wife, and his many collections. Houdini loved books; when traveling, he insisted on carrying hundreds with him, and at home a full-time curator tended the library. Houdini also collected unusual locks and handcuffs, magic memorabilia, autographs, and oddities such as Edgar Allen Poe's portable writing desk and an electric chair.

Stunts

Houdini spent much of his time at home perfecting new publicity stunts and acts for his show. He was determined to avoid slipping from the public eye, and he knew that failure to find fresh material meant the ultimate insult—being second on the bill.

One publicity stunt involved escaping from a straitjacket while hanging upside down from the top ledge of a building. The actual escape required only a few minutes, but Houdini usually played it out for fifteen or twenty minutes to maximize suspense. Naturally, crowds and traffic jams gathered for blocks around—exactly the sort of public uproar Houdini loved.

Perhaps his most famous stage act was the "Chinese Water Torture Cell." With hands shackled and feet enclosed in a wooden "stock," Houdini would be lowered upside down into a glass tank filled with water. The top was securely fastened, and assistants stood dramatically by with fire axes, prepared to break the glass if Houdini failed to escape. He never did.

Many escapes were performed behind a screen that hid Houdini from the audience. He might need only a few minutes to escape from a particular set of shackles. However, he would routinely stay behind the curtain for half an hour, reading a book as a band played tunes and the audience's anxiety gradually mounted. When the audience's distress was at a peak, he would appear from

Houdini engineers one of his dramatic escapes from a straitjacket while hanging upside down from a crane.

behind the screen with his clothes and hair mussed, feigning (pretending) exhaustion, as if he had been struggling nonstop.

Most of Houdini's escapes relied on genuine strength, agility, and stamina, and he constantly worked to improve these. He practiced holding his breath for long periods in an oversized bathtub. He performed card manipulations, without looking, while reading. He tied and untied knots with his toes while talking with friends. His most important secret, Houdini once wrote, was "vigorous self-training, to enable me to do remarkable things with my body, to make . . . every muscle . . . quick and sure for its part, to make my fingers super-fingers in dexterity, and to train my toes to do the work of fingers." [52]

But Houdini sometimes relied also on "gaffing," or rigging, his equipment. Bess might pass him tiny tools while kissing him for good luck before a stunt. An assistant might transfer a key with a handshake. Houdini also could conceal tools in parts of his body that passed the closest inspections. And if a prison escape was planned, Houdini or a confederate (an accomplice) often visited beforehand, providing an opportunity to make an impression of a key or drop tools into a crack in the floor.

Movies and Wartime

For a time before World War I, Houdini flirted with making movies. He saw silent film as a means of reaching vast new audiences, as well as a way of creating illusions impossible to present onstage.

In a handful of silent movies, Houdini acted as his own stunt-man in addition to writing scripts, choosing locations, starring,

Houdini, shown here with actress Mito Naldi, had a brief, unsuccessful movie career due to his stiff acting and inability to kiss his leading ladies.

directing, editing, and even handling publicity. He was not, however, a huge success with the filmgoing public; his tremendous on-stage charisma did not translate to film. He was done in primarily by his wooden acting; embarrassed to kiss his leading ladies, for instance, Houdini kept glancing at Bess off-camera.

Forced to admit defeat, Houdini closed his film production studio after only a few years. Biographer Ruth Brandon writes, "It was clear, even to Houdini, that although [film] might be the wave of the future, he would not be riding it. Houdini the film star embodied nobody's fantasies but his own."[53]

Too old for military service during the war, Houdini performed free for soldiers, and he organized benefits for the war effort. During this period, Houdini also began shifting the emphasis of his shows away from the strenuous escapes that had been his hallmark.

Part of the reason for this was simply the physical demands of his shows; Houdini's body was no longer as sturdy and resilient as it once had been. Another factor involved changing tastes. Weary, war-torn audiences were not looking for dangerous thrills; they did not want to see brushes with death when there was so much real death in the world every day. They preferred seeing light comedy, romance, and sentiment.

Houdini's shows began reflecting this, emphasizing traditional magic and illusions revived from previous shows. One example was the "Vanishing Elephant." Houdini performed this trick on several occasions and then stopped, jokingly citing wartime rationing. "I made two disappear a day," he later wrote. "That is twelve a week. [President] Hoover said that I was exhausting the elephant supply of the world."[54]

Love-Hate

The dominant aspect of Houdini's career after the war was his crusade to expose phony "spirit mediums."

Houdini had an intense love-hate relationship with spiritualism. He desperately wanted to communicate with his beloved mother, who had died in 1913. According to legend, he also formed solemn pacts with his wife, close friends, and associates. The first to die was to try to contact the survivors from beyond the grave.

At the same time, Houdini knew far too much about fooling a gullible and susceptible public. He became part of a distinguished committee, organized by *Scientific American* magazine, that took part in many high-profile investigations into psychic claims. He also maintained a standing offer, never claimed, of ten thousand dollars to anyone who could create a psychic phenomenon that he himself could not reproduce.

A worthy opponent for Houdini in the debate over spiritualism was Sir Arthur Conan Doyle, the famed creator of Sherlock Holmes. Conan Doyle passionately believed in spiritualism and insisted that Houdini was himself a powerful psychic unaware of his own remarkable powers. For a time the two famous men and their wives became friends, but eventually their differences forced them apart in a much-publicized rift.

Nothing else in Houdini's career created more controversy than his antipsychic crusade. Walter B. Gibson writes, "It is difficult today to picture the stir that Houdini's activities fomented [stirred up]. The wave of spiritualism that followed World War I had been fanned to the proportions of a tempest. . . . In taking the opposite side of the question, Houdini automatically plunged himself into something more than a controversy; namely, a full-fledged career." [55]

The Final Show

Houdini's death did not occur onstage, as legend has it. Nonetheless, it was as strange as any other event in his life.

In the fall of 1926, while with her husband on tour in New England, Bess suffered food poisoning. Houdini stayed up with her for several nights running while continuing his daily performance schedule. Then he injured himself onstage, breaking an ankle but stubbornly finishing the show.

In Montreal, the exhausted and injured performer invited three university students to visit him backstage between shows. He was relaxing on a couch, sorting through mail while chatting, when one student, an amateur boxer, asked Houdini if it was true that he could receive a blow anywhere above the belt except the face. Could he withstand a punch in the stomach?

Houdini, only half-listening, nodded and started to rise. Before the conjuror could tighten his stomach muscles—which would have prevented serious injury—the student struck him three times in the abdomen. The combination of exhaustion and the blows was too much. Houdini fell back and the color drained from his face. The students were horrified, but Houdini reassured them and ushered them out.

Houdini performed that afternoon, but by evening his stomach injury was very painful. The next day he experienced chills and sweats. On the train to Detroit that night, Houdini's assistant wired ahead to have a doctor at the station.

Houdini (left) and Sir Arthur Conan Doyle (right) held opposing views on spiritualism; Conan Doyle wholeheartedly believed in psychic powers while Houdini passionately decried them.

The physician announced that Houdini's appendix had ruptured, but Houdini refused to cancel his sold-out Detroit show. He made it through the show but collapsed immediately afterward. "There is such a thing as too much courage," biographer William Lindsay Gresham writes of this performance, "and Houdini showed it now. From the front, the audience could hardly suspect [that] they were watching a dying man." [56]

Houdini had advanced peritonitis, the inflammation that accompanies appendicitis. Doctors operated, but in the era before antibiotics this diagnosis was a death sentence. The escape king clung to life for a few more days before dying on October 31, 1926. His last words, spoken to his brother Hardeen, were, "Dash, I'm getting tired and I can't fight any more." [57]

After Death

Two thousand people attended Houdini's memorial service in New York, with hundreds of thousands more jamming the streets outside.

Until this occasion, the Society of American Magicians (SAM)—of which Houdini had long served as president—had no formal funeral rites. With the passing of their most famous member, however, the group created a ceremony that has been used, in modified form, at funerals for its members ever since. A cedar wand was broken and members recited a moving prayer.

Many rumors soon circulated about Houdini's death. Was the man who struck the fatal blow really a student? Was there

Houdini, pictured here with his wife, Bess, desperately wanted to communicate with his deceased mother, Cecelia Weiss.

something sinister behind his attack? The insurance company that had insured Houdini's life investigated but found no suspicion of foul play.

In the years after her husband's death, Bess tried running a tearoom, returned briefly to show business, and late in life moved to Los Angeles. She held a quiet séance on every anniversary of Houdini's death, hoping in vain to hear from him. Bess died in 1943, apparently with no desire to communicate from beyond the grave. "When I go, I'll be gone for good," she told friends. "I won't even try to come back." [58]

Houdini's legend today is a mixture of the human and the superhuman. His scrapbooks are on file at the Library of Congress. His enormous collections of handcuffs, magic apparatus, and other memorabilia are scattered among private collections and the Houdini Magical Hall of Fame in Niagara Falls, Ontario.

But these are tangible items; the intangible legends also remain, fueled by the eerie coincidence of his death occurring on Halloween. One of these persistent tales is that Houdini took a mysterious, all-powerful secret of the cosmos to the grave. Others tell stories of buried codes and hidden clues in the stones and inscriptions of his gravestone.

And so his name lives on. Even in death, after many years, Houdini remains the world's most famous illusionist.

CHAPTER 6

Jasper Maskelyne: The War Magician

Jasper Maskelyne, heir to a long and distinguished line of British conjurors, was literally born to magic when he came into the world in 1902.

His sixteenth-century ancestor, John Maskelyne, according to legend, made a pact with a sorcerer known as the Drummer of Tedworth. John Maskelyne sold his soul to purchase the powers of black magic for himself and his next ten generations.

More Maskelynes

Black magic or not, there were many notable Maskelynes in succeeding generations.

Nevil Maskelyne, the third generation after John, was, as King George III's royal astronomer, the first scientist to measure time to within tenths of a second, accurately calculate the weight of the Earth, and make other important discoveries about time and the stars.

The eighth generation brought John Nevil Maskelyne (1839–1917), the first professional magician in the family. He was one of the most famous illusionists of his day and a serious rival to Robert-Houdin for the title of "Father of Modern Magic."

John Nevil turned an obscure London venue into his professional home for thirty years: the Egyptian Hall, "England's Home of Mystery." He founded an elite magicians' organization, the Magic Circle, and wrote a classic book about conjuring, *Our Magic*.

He also created many famous and much-imitated illusions, including the "Box Trick," in which two people seemingly change places in an instant, and "Eye of the Needle," in which a person seemingly passes through a tiny hole in a steel plate. He caused full-bodied talking spirits to materialize from his own body, and he invented Psycho, a mechanical marvel that played flawless cards.

John Nevil's son Nevil Maskelyne (1863–1924) followed the tradition, performing his own show at Egyptian Hall for many

John Nevil Maskelyne, Jasper's grandfather, was one of the most famous illusionists of the nineteenth century.

years. Nevil's two sons, Noel and Jasper, both became magicians as well, but it was Jasper who found lasting fame.

The Boy Magician

Jasper's childhood years were spent surrounded by and learning the trappings of magic and wonder at his family's London home, at their country retreat in Kent, and backstage. There appears to have been little doubt that he would follow in the family tradition.

When not studying the world of illusion, the boy watched his father experiment with a dangerous but exciting hobby. Jasper noted in his memoirs that his father

> amused himself whenever he could spare time away from his stage-magic inventions and experiments [with] the manufacture of rockets and fire balloons. He used to make fire balloons six feet or more across, send them up in stately splendour from the Kentish fields, and let them drift at their own will. Attached were labels promising a reward to anyone who notified us, returning the label, of the place of descent. Some reached Scotland, others Germany, France, and Denmark. How I loved watching them sail silently away into the distant sky![59]

Jasper made his stage debut at the age of nine, in 1911, but he worked primarily backstage until 1926, when his father died. Then, at the age of twenty-four, Jasper Maskelyne stepped into the spotlight.

War Looms

Maskelyne was tall—six feet four inches—and handsome, with glossy hair and a thin moustache in the style favored then by movie idols. His stage show was similarly polished. Immediately after his adult debut, Maskelyne began performing regularly at the family's theater, as well as serving as its managing director. He was a hit both in London and abroad, thanks to tours of the Continent and Australia.

He was aided by his wife, Mary, whom he had met when the family hired her in 1925 as an assistant. In addition to raising their two children, Mary designed Maskelyne's elaborate sets, kept the company books, and was still occasionally called on to be shot out of a cannon or "disappeared" from a box onstage.

In the late 1930s, as hostilities in Europe built toward open war, the magician's first attempts to enlist in the British army were failures. Maskelyne knew his magic skills could be useful, but military authorities were skeptical. In his memoirs, the magician wrote, "I knew the way to produce the magic, but it was quite another thing to persuade the authorities at the War Office, the Admiralty, and the Air Ministry . . . to believe for one moment that I would be any use to them."[60]

Finally, a family friend arranged an interview with a high authority: the assistant to Prime Minister Winston Churchill.

According to David Fisher, Maskelyne gave the assistant a vivid picture of the possibilities:

> Given a free hand, there are no limits to the effects I can produce on the battlefield. I can create cannon where they don't exist and make ghost ships sail the seas. I can put an entire army in the field if you'd like, or make airplanes invisible, even project an image of Hitler sitting on the loo [toilet] a thousand feet into the sky.[61]

As a child, Jasper Maskelyne would watch in amazement as his father, Nevil, experimented with fire balloons like this one.

Antiaircraft fire lights up the sky over Algiers during a Nazi air raid.
Jasper Maskelyne was sent to war-torn North Africa in October 1940 to
help the Allies locate an evacuation route.

Fooling the Imam

In October 1940, the army appointed Maskelyne a reserve officer.
After a period at the Royal Engineers Camouflage Training and
Development Centre in rural Surrey, he was sent to the North
African desert, where British forces were battling Hitler's power-
ful Afrika Korps.

Maskelyne's first job was to outwit another conjuror, an effort
eerily like the one Robert-Houdin had done in Algeria. A particular tribe of desert dwellers controlled land that the Britons needed
for an evacuation route from Cairo, Egypt. However, the tribe's
Imam (leader) was reluctant to cooperate.

The Imam was proud of his supposed magical powers, and
when Maskelyne met with him they had a duel: the Imam levitated a carpet, Maskelyne fired a bullet through his hand, and the
contest continued back and forth. The Imam climaxed his performance by seemingly ramming a spear through his body without injury.

But Maskelyne proved the trick involved a leather belt that
turned the flexible spear aside, and he threatened to expose the
Imam. The Imam, wary of being seen as a fraud by his people, re-
luctantly guaranteed the Britons their request. Maskelyne noted

later that if he agreed "never to disclose that the old wangler was no more than a plain conjuror imposing on [tribal] credulity . . . he assured me that my mission would prove a complete success." [62]

British authorities in Cairo had been skeptical of Maskelyne, but this success gave him the credentials to form his own unit, the Camouflage Experimental Section. Fourteen men with unusual skills composed the unique team; in civilian life, they had held such jobs as motion picture stuntman, perfume specialist, optician, comic book illustrator, woodworker, stained-glass craftsman, electrical engineer, analytical chemist, stage-scenery manufacturer, pottery worker, and fine artist.

The Magic Gang

This motley group was soon dubbed the Magic Gang or Crazy Gang. Maskelyne was concerned less with their military training than their abilities; as he noted, "I was looking for people with initiative and ideas. . . . I cared little for discipline if I got genius." [63]

An entire valley near Cairo was eventually given over to Maskelyne for use as space for workshops, testing facilities, and living quarters. Magic Valley, as it was known, was heavily guarded with minefields and guardhouses, as well as such unconventional Maskelyne-devised traps as mirror mazes and trip wires that triggered recordings of terrifying sounds.

In the beginning, however, space, money, and materials were scarce. The team's first assignment was to produce, quickly and using only readily available materials, ten thousand gallons of desert camouflage paint. This was to cover 238 tanks that had recently arrived in Cairo painted forest green.

The Magic Gang proved to have a knack for scavenging Cairo's scrap heaps, Maskelyne noted: "You never in your life met such a set of men for scrounging the materials we needed for our work." [64] They uncovered hundreds of gallons of Worcestershire sauce, which Philip Townsend, the fine artist, combined with flour, cement dust, and other materials to create impromptu paint.

The right color was found by mixing in camel droppings. These were highly prized by Arabs as fuel, however, and were surprisingly difficult to find. A Magic Gang member invented a laxative for camels in an attempt to create more, but Maskelyne disallowed it: "I had to draw the line somewhere." [65]

Hiding the Harbor

The team also disguised convoys of tanks as harmless trucks. Maskelyne designed collapsible wooden frames with stretched and painted cloth, which clamped on either side of a tank. Each frame weighed thirty pounds and could be put in place by two men. The resulting silhouettes successfully fooled German air reconnaissance.

Far more complex was the task of camouflaging a crucial stronghold, Alexandria harbor, from daily air raids. Major Geoffrey Barkas, Maskelyne's superior officer, gave the magician his assignment: "I want you to hide that place so well that even [Egyptian king] Farouk in a bloody rowboat couldn't find it." [66]

The harbor's outline was familiar to German bombers. It had a distinctive shape, and at its entrance lay Pharos Island with its famous lighthouse. Complicating matters were the dozens of distinctive boats in the harbor and the many buildings and vehicles on land.

Maskelyne decided to make it appear that the entire harbor had moved. The magician thought he could produce a substitution on an enormous scale, by fooling German bombers into attacking another harbor, Maryut, which had a similar shape and which lay about a mile away. Working secretly, his team made the land around Maryut resemble Alexandria, using a complex network of

Wartime required great resourcefulness and improvisation, as exhibited by this variation of the rabbit-in-the-hat trick performed for members of the Magic Gang.

ground lights and fake buildings. The famous lighthouse was reproduced with a jerry-rigged replica. Phony ships of canvas and lights were placed in the harbor to create the impression that it was full of vessels.

The illusion was crude and would never have succeeded in daytime or up close. However, it was good enough to fool aircraft at night. The German pilots' instruments indicated that they were not precisely over Alexandria, but they took the visual bait and bombed the wrong target every night for a week.

The week's raid was the last large-scale German effort to shut down Alexandria. Thanks to Maskelyne and his team, British supplies and troops could continue to land there safely.

This and other illusions of Maskelyne's caught the attention of Adolf Hitler. The führer, a great believer in the occult, placed a substantial bounty on Maskelyne's head but publicly ridiculed the use of magic in warfare. A German newspaper, the *Berliner Illustrierte Zeitung*, noted, "The British have realised their situation is desperate and have employed a famous magician, Jasper Maske-

Smoke rises over Maryut after a Nazi air raid. Maskelyne successfully disguised Maryut's harbor to resemble Alexandria, the Nazi's intended target.

lyne, to try to scare off the Afrika Korps! . . . Indeed, the Führer told Tank General Rommel, the German Army does not need a Maskelyne to make the British Army disappear."[67]

Hiding Suez

An even more spectacular stunt was hiding the Suez Canal. This vital waterway, the link between the Mediterranean and Red Seas, was controlled by the British. They knew that Hitler would not destroy it, since he needed it. More likely, they felt, the Germans would temporarily block the narrow passage by sinking a ship from the air, then wait until it was in German hands before restoring it. Here was an illusion on a truly grand scale. How could Maskelyne hide 107 miles of canal, with nothing but flat desert on either side?

Using scale models, he toyed with the idea of mirrors but decided he could make only sections of it disappear. He also experimented with distorting its location by changing shadows across the ground, but he abandoned that idea as requiring too much specialized equipment.

The solution came by accident, when Maskelyne was temporarily blinded by a colleague who accidentally directed a bright light in his face. He realized that he might be able to blind and confuse bomber pilots, even in daylight, with a huge curtain of light. "Without light," Maskelyne later wrote, "the eye is useless; [but] light skilfully used can create the most astounding deceptions and effects."[68]

High-powered beacons were in short demand; Maskelyne needed to increase the power of the ones on hand. This was done with reflectors. Maskelyne and his crew designed an arrangement of reflectors that divided each beacon's light into twenty-four separate beams. Each beam was capable of covering nearly the same area of the sky as the original, as much as nine miles across, and with nearly the same intensity. A further modification set the reflectors spinning, creating a dazzling cartwheel of light.

Testing involved Maskelyne and other observers, including a professor of light physics at the University of Cairo, flying into the curtain of light made by one of these super reflectors. The effect was like a stunning blow in the face, and the pilots of both test planes became so disoriented that they nearly lost control of their crafts. After an emergency landing, Maskelyne was briefly hospitalized. He wryly commented in a letter to his wife, "We had a rough time of it in the air testing out something I invented. Perhaps you were right about all this flying business being dangerous."[69]

In an effort to hide the Suez Canal, Maskelyne modified beacons like this one with reflectors to create a blinding burst of light that would disorient Nazi bombers.

Twenty-one superlights eventually spanned the length of the canal. Several attempts were made by the Germans to bomb the canal, but Maskelyne's system proved too disorienting. The canal remained in British hands.

Spy Tools

As the war progressed, Maskelyne was also asked to create tools on a much smaller scale, for use by British soldiers and espionage agents.

He found that the tongue of a boot could be modified to conceal maps, and its side flaps could hold a hacksaw. Razors or toothbrushes could cloak escape kits, each including a nail puller, hacksaw, screwdriver, wire cutter, wrench, compass, and two edible maps made of rice paper. Tiny magnetized compass needles could be concealed in the aglet (the tiny piece at the end of a shoelace), in pipe stems, or in collar stays.

Saw blades capable of cutting iron were concealed as identification disc chains worn around the neck, or as watchbands, key chains, or good luck charms. A cigarette holder held a telescope, a fountain pen became a tear gas dispenser. For soldiers in India and Burma, Maskelyne developed an innocent-looking sliver of bamboo that, when tossed in water, became a compass. He noted in his memoirs, "A Japanese sentry might actually watch a prisoner idly toss such a thing out of his pocket, and never dream that the man was taking a compass bearing for a forthcoming escape." [70]

Tens of thousands of Maskelyne's spy tools were issued to British soldiers during the war. For each invention, Maskelyne received only the army's standard five-pound bonus.

"Maskelyne in Your Area"

Maskelyne was also pressed into service on the sea. Among other projects, he and his crew created a fleet of spy boats disguised as slow-moving working ships and/or millionaires' yachts. Each had carefully created but entirely false logbooks and records, and crew members (many of them Greek allies) had painstakingly detailed false identities.

A spy vessel could sail into German-controlled areas of the Mediterranean as one ship, pass inspection, then change to a completely new disguise while hidden in a patch of sea mist and emerge with a completely new identity. More than twenty of these ships successfully delivered and picked up undercover agents and cargo up and down the Mediterranean.

The Magic Gang also created dummy submarine fleets. German reconnaissance planes flew over British sub bases in the Mediterranean every two hours to count vessels. British authorities reasoned that if dummy subs were substituted for real ones, real ones could leave undetected. Full-size, easily transportable fakes were thus devised, using old railway cars as buoyant frames. The prototype built by the Magic Gang was named HMS *Hopeful* because its designers were not entirely sure it would float.

During testing, the admiral in charge of the Cairo region received intelligence concerning an unidentified sub. Knowing it was not his, he nearly ordered it destroyed. Maskelyne had to disobey

This phony wooden tank was designed as part of an entire fake army for the purpose of misleading the Nazis.

strict secrecy orders to keep his project safe, and the admiral received the following message from high up the command chain: REGRET MISUNDERSTANDING BUT MASKELYNE IN YOUR AREA OTHER TRANSFORMATIONS WILL BE TAKING PLACE. [71]

An Entire Fake Army

Maskelyne pulled off an enormous bluff, concealing an entire army while creating a false one, as part of the Battle of El Alamein, one of the decisive battles of the desert war.

The Britons needed to convince the Germans that they were preparing an attack along one flank of their defenses when in fact it was planned for the other. Maskelyne's task was to conceal a massive buildup of real troops, supplies, and weapons in one area while creating the illusion of a buildup elsewhere. As in a classic stage misdirection, everything had to appear to be in plain view. It was crucial that German observers see a large group of harmless transport and supply vehicles in one area, with the armored forces apparently headed elsewhere.

Fakes were built that would never have fooled anyone up close, but were realistic enough to fool airplanes taking photos. Dummy supply caches were made from palm-wood bed frames, pickets, dummy railroad tracks, old fuel cans, wicker tomato cases, wire, and netting. Real campfires were lit at night outside dummy tents. Fake tanks and other vehicles made the compound seem more plausible. Special crews moved the dummy soldiers around and created new tire tracks so that the scene would appear different every day.

Thousands of dummy soldiers made of canvas and cardboard, apparently running or walking or napping, "manned" this supply compound. Real uniforms were used when available; otherwise they were painted. The Magic Gang created some dummies with especially large bellies stuffed with cloth and called them "sergeants."

At the last moment, the Britons performed a transposition, with real forces moving quickly in and the attack staged where it was not expected. El Alamein was an enormous victory for the Britons, in large part due to the Magic Gang's camouflage efforts. The actual transposition took only two days, and the German forces were devastated. Prime Minister Winston Churchill, addressing Britain's House of Commons, stated,

> By a marvelous system of camouflage, complete tactical surprise was achieved in the desert. The enemy suspected—indeed, knew—that an attack was impending, but when and where and how it was coming was hidden from him. The Tenth Corps, which had been seen from the air exercising fifty miles in the rear, moved silently away in the night, leaving an exact simulacrum [replica] of its tanks where it had been and proceeding to its points of attack.[72]

Station M and Retirement

Maskelyne was promoted to major after this victory, but the Magic Gang broke up.

For a time the magician was stationed at the British army's spy center, Station M, on the shores of Canada's Lake Ontario. (Station M was part of a larger complex known as Camp X.) From this base, Maskelyne flew around the world to devise increasingly sophisticated illusions. Writer William Stevenson reports, "The 'M' in Station M was said to stand for Magic and [for] Jasper Maskelyne, a hero to British schoolboys before the war, one of the great magicians of all time and a master at the art of deception."[73]

Maskelyne returned to England at the war's end, after seven years in uniform, and was at last able to return to a smaller stage. "We were all desperately anxious to get home and see our families again," he noted in his memoirs. "My mind was seething with new ideas by which, reversing the former process, I could now transform war-magic into stage-magic." [74]

Unfortunately, he had little success in reviving his stage show; audiences no longer seemed interested. In 1948, the Maskelynes migrated to Kenya, fulfilling the magician's longtime dream of retiring to a farm. There, he worked for the national police during its war against the Mau Mau, managed the Kenya National Theatre, gave occasional performances, and wrote his memoirs. The magician whose skills changed the course of a world war died on his farm near Nairobi in 1973.

CHAPTER 7

David Copperfield: "The First Pop Idol of Prestidigitation"

Vaudeville theater began declining as a popular entertainment in the 1920s and 1930s, as movies and other diversions rose in popularity. Magicians had long relied on these vaudeville houses as a steady means of employment. As vaudeville died, magic fell into a slump; fewer and fewer people, it seemed, were interested in seeing conjuring on a stage.

Not even the powerful medium of television, which became widespread in the 1950s, could help revive the art. Partly, this was because viewers thought trick photography might be at work. Writers Lisa Gubernick and Peter Newcomb comment, "Except for the occasional Ed Sullivan spot, there was little magic on the small screen; television audiences couldn't be convinced that the illusions were created by the magicians and not the camera." [75]

Riding the Revival

In the early 1970s, faddish New Age attitudes toward the occult helped spark a revival in magic. The most popular conjuror during this period was a Canadian-born performer, Doug Henning, whose appearance featured shoulder-length hair and flowing, tie-dyed clothes. Henning's looks struck a responsive chord in audiences, according to a noted magic consultant, Charles Reynolds: "The really successful magicians are the ones who are able to resonate with their audiences. . . . Henning was one with his audiences, the flower children, the hippies. He somehow convinced them that he really believed [in magic]." [76]

It looked for a period as though Henning would assume the mantle of Houdini, and the younger magician even wrote a brief biography of the master. However, Henning became involved with an Indian spiritual teacher, the Maharishi Mahesh Yogi, and

Conjuror Doug Henning's New Age antics gained him immense popularity with television audiences during the 1970s.

dropped out of show business. Another man was destined to become the preeminent magician of the late twentieth century, succeeding thanks to a canny combination of show-biz savvy, commercial instincts, and a genuine gift for conjuring.

David Copperfield is, by almost any reckoning, the most popular illusionist alive. More people have seen him perform than any other magician, present or past. He has made an enormous fortune from his skills. And, by combining traditional magic and illusion with modern flash, he has become the most important living heir to the kind of large-scale, crowd-pleasing shows perfected by classic performers like Houdini and Kellar.

There are, of course, many other gifted contemporary magicians who also carry on this tradition. James Randi (the Amazing Randi), Harry Blackstone Jr., and the duo of Siegfried and Roy are only a few of the best known. No one, however, has done it on a larger scale, or more extravagantly, than Copperfield. He is, states writer Bill Zehme, "the first pop idol of prestidigitation and, more significantly, Houdini's only logical heir." [77]

Teen Star

David Seth Kotkin was born in 1956 and grew up in Metuchen, New Jersey. He is the only child of Rebecca and Hyman Kotkin, the owners of a clothing store.

By all accounts, David's childhood was quite normal for a middle-class kid of the late 1950s and 1960s. However, he was shy, and a desire to impress girls sparked an early interest in

David Copperfield has become the most popular large-scale illusionist since Houdini.

performance. First planning to be a ventriloquist, he was diverted to magic when he visited a magic shop to buy a ventriloquist's dummy.

He taught himself magic, started performing before he turned ten (mostly for other kids at parties), and by his early teens was displaying a precocious talent. He became the youngest person ever to be admitted into the Society of American Magicians (SAM), and by sixteen was teaching magic courses at New York University.

Early on, he also showed an interest in the theater. By his own admission, David hated high school and seized every opportunity to visit the theater instead:

> I'd rush into New York every day from New Jersey and sneak into Broadway shows. I would second-act them—that's what they call it when you sneak into shows during intermission. I'd slip into the theater bathroom during the break and wait till just after intermission when everyone was seated. Then I'd take a seat. I saw all of [theatrical giants] Bob Fosse's and Stephen Sondheim's and Jerome Robbins's work, but only the second halves.[78]

In high school, Copperfield was a shy teen who disliked school but loved performing and the theater. When his senior yearbook picture was taken, young Copperfield was already teaching magic courses at New York University.

Still in his teens, David played the lead in a musical production, "The Magic Man," which was mounted in Chicago. Spotted by a television producer in 1977, he created a series of ads to promote ABC's new fall shows. When he was nineteen, a rival network, CBS, offered him his own special. He has starred in an annual special for the network ever since, winning the magician a huge audience and a number of Emmys.

Along the way, David adopted as his stage name that of the title character in Charles Dickens's novel *David Copperfield*. The magician admits that he has never managed to finish Dickens's lengthy classic. "Even the Cliffs Notes aren't that interesting," he says, adding that he found the film version "kind of dark."[79]

Live!

Copperfield's television specials are famous for the enormous scale of their illusions. He has walked through the Great Wall of China, flown across the Grand Canyon, and made the Statue of Liberty and a seven-ton jet airliner vanish into thin air. He has also performed a number of flamboyant escapes: from a flaming raft over Niagara Falls, from shackles while suspended over hundreds of flaming metal stakes, from the maximum-security prison of Alcatraz, and from within an imploding skyscraper.

His live shows, however, remain an important part of Copperfield's career. The magician and his crew of about forty assistants mount more than five hundred performances a year in a grueling round-the-world schedule.

In some ways, the live shows are even more important to Copperfield than his television specials, since they keep his skills sharp by putting him in front of a demanding live audience year-round. He comments, "I love performing and it will always be a staple of my career. Magic is a live medium. That's where it works best." [80]

As is true of many entertainers, when Copperfield began his career he was a stiff and almost nerdy performer. His persona has changed dramatically, however,

Copperfield's polished onstage performances—the result of years in the entertainment industry—are often likened to those of a rock star.

and over the years he has come to personify something very different: the magician as rock star. Copperfield summarizes this persona by saying, "The structure of the show is me posing, looking really cool, and having girls wrapped around me." [81]

Writer Joanna Powell describes the opening of a typical Copperfield performance:

> The lights go down to the tune of Aerosmith's "Love in an Elevator," and Copperfield suddenly materializes in a stage elevator that was empty just seconds before. . . .

Copperfield vamps around the stage, a long, lean silhouette in painted-on-tight black Levi's, black cowboy boots, and a crisp white shirt with gold buttons designed exclusively for him by Gianni Versace. . . . With his thick dark hair, haunting brown eyes, and fresh glowing tan, Copperfield is dashing—in a tiger-trainer kind of way.[82]

Drama

The magician typically follows this dramatic entrance with his own variations on classic illusions, including the "Death Saw," in which Copperfield appears to be cut in half; one in which he flies like an eagle over the audience; and a mind-reading act called the "Graffiti Wall." But the centerpieces of a Copperfield show are his trademark minidramas. These are romantic fantasies—often set to pulsating music by rockers like Peter Gabriel and Terence Trent D'Arby—that combine theater with magic.

Magic scholar T. A. Waters feels that Copperfield is at his best in this context, "when he integrates television technique with music, choreography, and a story line [into] first-class entertainment."[83] Copperfield feels that his minidramas reflect his love of theater, noting that he wants to "achieve that same level of emotion [as the best theater] using an art form that I really loved. I [want] to make magic move the audience in the same way that I was being moved on Broadway."[84]

One powerful minidrama is Copperfield's standard finale, in which he produces snow from between his bare hands. The snow fills the entire theater, and Copperfield transforms himself into a little boy as he tells the audience of his childhood fascination with snow. He comments,

Snow was the first thing that I witnessed as a kid that I didn't immediately understand. It had a magical quality—this white stuff fell from the sky, and a whole scene change took place. So something that seems so unremarkable to me today was very magical to me then.[85]

Magic and Wealth

Copperfield's formula has been so successful that he is one of the wealthiest entertainers alive, with earnings in the tens of millions annually. His wealth has enabled the illusionist to buy a number of unusual and even outrageous items. One of these is his twenty-thousand-square-foot office-workshop in the desert near Las Vegas, Nevada, where he often performs in the many casinos.

Copperfield claims to have no real home, since he is on the road so much, but the Las Vegas locale serves as his de facto home.

In designing his hideaway, Copperfield indulged in some of his love of secrets. Located in an old nuts-and-bolts warehouse, the retreat is concealed behind a phony bra-and-girdle showroom; access to his inner sanctum is gained by way of a secret sliding mirror. Writer Bill Zehme characterizes it as being "like the Batcave, only with less furniture and no kitchen."[86]

In addition to serving as an office (Copperfield runs much of his business empire by himself), this secret lair stores equipment for more than 250 of his illusions. It also houses a priceless collection of thousands of historic magic-related artifacts, books, and posters, including props once used by Houdini, Robert-Houdin, and Thurston. This is believed to be the largest private collection of magic memorabilia in the world.

Copperfield's wealth also allows him to purchase such items as the Batmobile created for the 1989 movie *Batman*. The magician wanted to bid anonymously for the car, and had decided to pay no more than $150,000. However, it was auctioned in Los Angeles while the magician was performing in North Carolina. Copperfield had a phone brought onstage and told the audience what he was doing. He recalls, "I had 4,000 people cheering, 'Go for it, David!' So I was in a bad negotiating position and paid $189,500."[87]

Magic and Modeling

For many years, Copperfield concentrated almost obsessively on perfecting his show and performing around the world. He dated many women but had no steady girlfriend. That changed in 1993, when he began a long-running and highly publicized romance with a German-born supermodel, Claudia Schiffer.

The two met in Berlin when they both appeared at a gala show that headlined Copperfield. The illusionist pulled Schiffer onstage to help him with his Graffiti Wall mind-reading act, and it was, by all accounts, love at first sight.

After a courtship of only four months, Copperfield proposed to Schiffer and presented her with a five-carat diamond engagement ring valued at $4.5 million. He has since bought her a number of other lavish gifts, including, for a reported $2 million, a luxury yacht called the *Honey Fitz*. (President John F. Kennedy once relaxed aboard the same yacht.)

So far, their romance has been conducted around the world. Schiffer lives in Monaco, Copperfield in Las Vegas, and both are constantly traveling for their work. The two meet when and where

David Copperfield (right) and longtime girlfriend, model Claudia Schiffer (left), pose with Copperfield's wax likeness at Madame Tussaud's in London.

they can, although they have adopted a rule: the longest they will go without rendezvousing is two weeks. Copperfield has also begun doubling up his performances, working harder in shorter bursts in order to spend more time with Schiffer. While apart, they remain in constant touch by telephone. He jokes: "Why do you think I do all these shows? To pay for the phone bills!"[88]

Love and Lawsuits

From all appearances, the pair are very close. However, the length of their engagement—six years and counting—has led to constant gossip and speculation that the relationship is on rocky ground. Schiffer says she tries to laugh off published rumors, but that it is not always easy.

> When a story says David or I was with someone else and one of our parents calls and asks, "Is it true?" it really hurts. You know they're home wondering about you. [But] we're enjoying ourselves. It's the first time either of us has been engaged, and it's a very different experience from just dating someone. So we're taking our time.[89]

Copperfield adds that he would like a family, but not until he and Schiffer are ready to slow their globe-trotting pace. He jokes, "We'll get married when people stop asking us when we're going to get married." [90]

In 1997, a scandalous report led to some unwelcome publicity and a multi-million-dollar lawsuit, still pending. It stemmed from an article published in a popular French magazine, *Paris Match*. The article charged that the couple's engagement was nothing more than an elaborate illusion—that the supermodel was paid for pretending to be Copperfield's fiancée and that, in fact, she disliked him.

Copperfield and Schiffer were so incensed by the *Paris Match* piece that they sued the magazine for thirty million dollars. *Time* magazine wryly commented about the fracas, "Here's a new trick David Copperfield's learning: if you can't make something disappear, sue the people who created it." [91]

Other Ventures

Besides his magic shows and his much-publicized romance, Copperfield has been involved in several other projects.

He is slowly working to make public some of his vast collection of magic memorabilia. He has plans to create an International Museum and Library of the Conjuring Arts, which will be available to serious scholars as well as to the general public.

In 1995, he coedited *Tales of the Impossible*, a collection of original short stories by such writers as Ray Bradbury, Joyce Carol Oates, and Dean Koontz. *Tales* also included a story by Copperfield called "Snow," an autobiographical account in which a boy discovers the magic of snow and his power to recreate it. The following year Copperfield coedited another book of short fiction, *Beyond Imagination*.

To promote interest in magic, Copperfield is planning to open a museum and library that will showcase magic artifacts such as this nineteenth-century three-lens magic lantern.

A more ambitious program is Project Magic, a program de-signed to help doctors and therapists use sleight of hand as ther-apy with patients who have damaged motor or cognitive (mental) skills. Sleight of hand, Copperfield feels, helps to increase a pa-tient's physical dexterity and coordination; it also boosts self-esteem, since magic is a skill that most able-bodied people do not possess. Copperfield comments, "The beauty of the magic is that it gives disabled people skills that the able-bodied don't have." [92]

Project Magic took shape in 1981, when Copperfield realized that a magician with whom he had been corresponding was dis-abled. Copperfield recalls, "He had never referred to the fact that he was in a wheelchair. I began thinking about the role magic might play in the lives of the disabled." [93]

The illusionist began working with an occupational therapist from the Daniel Freeman Memorial Hospital in Inglewood, Cali-fornia. Together they created a series of simple tricks, such as sus-pending a knife in midair and tying a knot that then disappears, that could be taught as part of regular therapy. Project Magic has since grown to include programs at hospitals in many states and countries.

Too Slick?

Some observers are critical of Copperfield's showy style, with its beautiful assistants, loud music, and fireworks. They argue that he is less a magician than a pop entertainer, that his shows are more style than substance. "Copperfield is essentially doing music videos with magic in them," says Teller, the usually silent half of the magic duo Penn and Teller. "He's clearly using MTV as the metaphor for his performance." [94]

However, Copperfield is unapologetic about this policy of com-bining magic with slick show-biz moves. He is also matter-of-fact about recycling his most popular illusions year after year, noting that they are the most financially rewarding: "I fly because there's a market for it." [95]

No one can deny the success of Copperfield's strategy. Even Penn Jillette, the sardonic other half of Penn and Teller, acknowl-edges Copperfield's commercial savvy: "All of [his commercial-ism] is very, very smart, and it works. He has learned how to make TV pay off, how to make it work together with his live perfor-mance. To be honest, if we were to follow the Copperfield rules of business, in terms of pure finance we'd be much better off." [96]

One criticism of Copperfield's slick style is that he sacrifices genuine emotion in his efforts to present a highly polished show.

A physical therapist works with a disabled woman. Copperfield established Project Magic to aid in the therapy of disabled people by teaching them sleight-of-hand tricks that can improve their dexterity and self-esteem.

Copperfield acknowledges the difficulty in putting across genuine emotion to large audiences, especially when high-tech equipment is used. A magician, he says, has to know a great deal about the technology and the techniques of magic. But, he warns,

> if an audience leaves a theater and all they are interested in is guessing at the secret behind one of the illusions, that would be like someone walking out of [a film] only discussing a great camera angle and not the story. For the technology to grow, it has to reach into people's hearts and use their emotions a little bit. . . . I like balancing out the big spectacular acts with things that are more intimate [and can] touch people, make them cry.[97]

Copperfield's showy style is at one end of the continuum of modern magic. At the other is that of Penn and Teller.

Penn and Teller: "A Couple of Eccentric Guys Who Have Learned a Few Cool Things"

Penn and Teller generally appear onstage in conservative business suits. Otherwise, they are a study in contrasts.

Penn is six feet six, hyperactive, and built like a football player, with unruly hair and a single fingernail painted red. He does almost no sleight of hand, magic, or juggling, though he is gifted at all of these. What he does is storm the audience with talk, a nonstop barrage of words that journalist Calvin Trillin calls "a constant, aggressive, consciously hip, often overbearing, occasionally hostile flow." [98]

Teller is nearly a foot shorter than his partner, with a cloud of wispy hair. Though he is highly articulate offstage, Teller almost never speaks while performing. Instead, he uses his expressive face to convey emotions. Teller does virtually all of the magic, and many observers of the current magic scene consider him one of the most gifted sleight-of-hand artists in the world.

Penn and Teller know that they could not achieve separately as much as they do together. Their separate traits and abilities, when combined, create something larger than the individual parts. "In some way, we're co-dependent," Penn says. "It's so charming, and so wonderfully reactionary, in a time when relationships last five years, for us to be partners [for more than twenty years]. We flaunt that we can't function without each other." [99]

Growing Up Big and Weird

Penn Jillette was born in 1955 and raised in Greenfield, Massachusetts. His father was a former prison guard (at the Franklin County Jail) turned numismatist, or coin collector. His mother

The outrageous duo of Penn (left) and Teller (right) has been entertaining audiences with its comedic magic for more than twenty years.

was a practical joker whose tricks included such stunts as waking him with tales of rhinos in the backyard.

By grade school, Penn was already something of a misfit. He was already taller than some of his teachers. Furthermore, his parents were far older than most of his friends' parents. His only sibling, a sister, was twenty-three years older than he.

Like many performers, Penn is fond of embellishing his life story. He sometimes tells reporters that he was kicked out of high school when in fact he graduated normally with good marks and was never in serious trouble. He did hang out with bad kids, but in high school (and ever since) he has studiously avoided alcohol and drugs. Penn's high-school rebelliousness seems to have been concentrated mainly on his appearance, which featured bold eye shadow, shocking clothes, and long hair. His longtime friend Marc Garland says,

> Penn was just outrageous. He had all this creative energy. He was out of his mind with ideas—maybe not even ideas, but ideas that he wanted to have ideas—and here he was stuck in this very straight, for him oppressive atmosphere. So he was the crazy: too loud, too much energy, too crazily dressed.[100]

Penn had long been drawn to performance, in part because the misfit could practice such activities as juggling and unicycling alone. Most of his nonschool hours were devoted to perfecting his skills in these areas.

His first public performance came soon after graduating from Greenfield High, in an amateur production staged in 1973 by college students in nearby Amherst, Massachusetts. As a musician played "The Star-Spangled Banner," Penn rode his unicycle and juggled across the stage.

Growing Up Small and Weird

One of the other performers in that show was a slight, studious graduate of Amherst College who was then teaching Latin at a high school in New Jersey and performing magic on weekends. This conjuror was already known by only his last name.

Teller (who has since legally changed his name to simply "Teller") was born in 1948 and grew up in central Philadelphia. An only child, he was, like Penn, born to older parents—in this case, a commercial artist and his wife, a fine artist.

Also like Penn, Teller was a misfit, though in his case the isolation stemmed from a quiet, shy nature. Even as a young boy, he spent hours alone in his room. After receiving a magic set at the age of five, Teller's future course was set. From then on, his father wryly says, "Handkerchiefs were always flying all over." [101]

As a boy, Teller put on occasional backyard carnivals featuring himself as a swami telling fortunes in his dog's house, and he built fun houses to scare and mystify neighbor kids. He recalls,

> There were odd pieces of wood in my back yard—things like long planks with four-by-fours nailed to the ends of them so as to form a small table. . . . I loved to take those things and put them in sequences, so that at each step something surprising . . . would happen—so, say, a plank would tip in a different direction. And then I would get kids who lived on my street to come in and walk through it. [In] my head what was happening was they were going into a fun house in an amusement park—a haunted house that was pretty scary. [102]

Teller was an accomplished amateur magician by the time he attended Central High, a Philadelphia school for high-aptitude students. He was already performing silently, without the safety net of a conventional magician's patter, because he found he could attract the attention of rowdy college students at parties more ef-

Clad in conservative wet "suits," Penn and Teller pose with a harpoon gun and huge saw, props from their 1989 movie Penn and Teller Get Killed.

fectively that way. Also, he says, he "became fascinated with the prospect of lying without speaking." [103]

In high school, Teller was deeply influenced by David Rosenbaum, the school's respected drama coach and an amateur magician. After graduating from college in 1969, Teller followed in his mentor's footsteps, teaching high school Latin while performing magic shows on weekends.

Asparagus Valley

When Penn and Teller met, the bond was not instant. Teller recalls, "We didn't start out liking each other, but we were interested in each other." Penn adds, "We had no affection for each other at all. But I found Teller to be the most inspired, well thought out and hardworking guy I'd ever met. . . . We didn't know anything, except what we wanted to see on stage." [104]

The two began to discuss regularly what they liked and hated about performance. Meanwhile, they continued to develop solo acts, on the street and at various fairs. This daily exposure in front of a tough, demanding audience honed their skills and helped in other ways. Teller perfected his eloquent face and body movements, and Penn assembled his ironic, aggressive persona. (When urging audiences to give generously after a street show, Penn would cheerfully tell them, "Remember: I'm six-six, I have three very sharp knives, and I have an excellent memory." [105])

In 1975, Teller cautiously took a leave of absence from his teaching job to join up full-time with Penn in a performance troupe. The third member of this group was musician Wier Chrisemer. The trio called themselves the Asparagus Valley Cultural Society, a name inspired by an area of western Massachusetts. The opening-night party for one of their early performances featured cookies baked by Teller's mother.

Jump for Life

To drum up publicity for one show, Penn staged his first notable failure: "Asparagus Penn's Unicycle Jump for Life," a parody of the daredevil motorcyclist Evel Knievel. Freely inventing scientific-sounding data for the media about what would happen when he reached top speed, the performer claimed that he would attempt to jump over five VW Rabbits while riding a rocket-powered unicycle.

Accounts vary as to exactly what happened, but apparently Penn fell off the ramp on his way into the air. Indignant drunks in the crowd then assaulted him and damaged the Rabbits, which had been loaned to the troupe by a local car dealer. Penn escaped serious injury by being rescued by an ambulance team that had been asked to stand by as a joke.

When Asparagus Valley's producer, James Freydberg, took the show to San Francisco, things improved. The troupe was a major hit, and the show ran for nearly three years.

Toward the end of this long run, in 1981, Freydberg suggested moving the show to New York. Wier was willing to go, but Penn and Teller were more interested in staying in San Francisco to work on a theater piece they were creating. When the troupe broke up, Wier returned to the East Coast and took a regular job. According to Teller, Wier was increasingly unhappy anyway with the long hours and uncertain fortunes of the theater world: "Wier wanted a life." [106]

During Comic Relief '89, Penn's aggressive demeanor and Teller's eloquent persona play in sharp contrast while trying to levitate a screaming Bobcat Goldthwait.

Penn and Teller Become "Penn & Teller"

Unfortunately, the new show, a highly intellectualized program called "Mrs. Lonsberry's Evening of Horror," was a flop. Penn and Teller returned to the fair-and-street circuit. In 1982, after years of working as solo acts with occasional pairings, they decided to begin working strictly as a team.

This act coalesced into their first full-length show, "Penn & Teller." The new show had marginally successful runs in many cities around the country. The venues the duo played were often run-down clubs. Sometimes only a handful of people were in the audience. Crisscrossing the country, the illusionists spent their nights sleeping in their beat-up white Datsun or in cheap motels.

The show typically opened with an act that has become a Penn & Teller staple. Teller is strapped into a straitjacket and suspended upside down above a bed of spikes. Penn sits casually in a chair that is attached to the rope holding Teller. Penn announces he will recite the poem "Casey at the Bat" and stand to accept applause when he is done. If Teller has not freed himself in time, he will plummet headfirst onto the spikes.

Another highlight of the show that is still a staple is a delicate illusion called "Shadows." A rose sits in a vase on a stand; behind it, projected on a white screen, is its shadow. Teller takes a pair of scissors to the silhouette of the rose, snipping away at the shadow; as he does, the petals fall from the real flower as if they have been snipped.

The show closed with Penn sitting alone in near darkness, swallowing fire and talking quietly about sideshow performers and life in general. "People get to know you by the end of the show," he explains. "Then you should be able to talk in quiet tones without jokes." [107]

The "Debunking Thang"

"Penn & Teller" was the prototype of future Penn and Teller shows, an amalgamation of illusions, tricks, and "bits" tied together with underlying themes. Perhaps their primary theme is a philosophy that champions science and rationality over mindless belief. As Penn often puts it, their shows are about "using your head in a world full of flim-flam." [108]

Another theme is one of mocking conventional magic shows. Penn emphasizes often in interviews that he and Teller dislike most magic and are themselves far from being "some greasy guys in tuxes with birds or some aging hippies who shove women into boxes." [109]

Penn and Teller's repertoire of illusions feature many stunts that threaten the duo with bodily harm. Here, the pair inspects a 450-pound refrigerator that will be dropped on them during a New York show.

The most extreme example of this theme is the pair's penchant for revealing how tricks are done. For instance, they will perform a classic sleight of hand, a shell game involving cups hiding balls, in the conventional way. They will then perform it again, using clear plastic cups.

Because Penn and Teller perform the stunt with dexterity and style, however, even when explained the trick remains mystifying.

Furthermore, inside knowledge only seems to increase the audience's pleasure. Critic Charles Isherwood writes, "Perhaps the biggest trick of all is how their gleeful embrace of the 'debunking thang,' as Penn calls it, serves only to enhance the appeal of classic tricks. . . . [S]howing us how a casual hide-the-cigarette illusion works doesn't deflate our opinion of their talents, it somehow enlarges it." [110]

The pair's "debunking thang" often involves illusions of their own invention as well. Teller comments, "With ordinary magic tricks it wouldn't be [as] interesting. So we invent a trick done by such clever methods it's worth revealing. Magic is a stimulating intellectual experience, and part of the delight is trying to figure out where reality leaves off and make believe begins." [111]

Tipping the Gaff

These explanations of how a trick is done—"tipping the gaff" in show-business parlance—have outraged many mainstream magicians. Many magicians have publicly complained that Penn and Teller are betraying a sacred tradition and undercutting other illusionists.

Penn and Teller are scornful of such criticism. They point out that little is actually given away in their act. Besides, they say, few spectators really care how a trick is done; they just want to be entertained. Journalist Calvin Trillin reflects the opinion of magic consultant Charles Reynolds when he writes, "In Charles's view, the magicians who become furious . . . have an outsized notion of how much people in the audience learn from having a trick explained to them, and how much they care." [112]

Penn and Teller further add that few magicians have invented genuinely new effects since the turn of the century; most illusions are adaptations of existing ideas. For instance, Teller's ability to swallow a hundred needles and then regurgitate them threaded is merely a variation of a trick performed by Houdini, who claimed he learned it from a Chinese conjuror in 1893. Penn comments that any decent library contains books detailing the secrets of famous tricks, and adds that more information is available on the Web: "Anybody that can use [an Internet search engine like] Yahoo! can find every single trick that was in Houdini's repertoire within, probably, 15 to 20 minutes." [113]

Stars

For a couple of years, Penn and Teller remained little more than underground sensations. Their big break came in 1985, during the duo's first appearance in New York.

The show, at an off-Broadway theater, was a runaway success. As word got out about the fresh, startling, outrageous new performers in town, Penn and Teller suddenly became the toast of New York, with celebrities vying for tickets to their sold-out shows. Typical of the critical reaction was this assessment by the *New Yorker*'s Edith Oliver:

> Everything the partners do has a style all its own. . . . There are feats of legerdemain and deception, all of them new to me and some of them dangerous, involving cards and coins, an apple and needles and thread, sharp knives, and fire-eating. . . . Time after time, one finds oneself gasping and laughing simultaneously.[114]

As the pair's reputation grew, a number of high-profile opportunities arose. They appeared on a *Saturday Night Live* episode hosted by Madonna. In the first of what became many performances on David Letterman's late-night show, they emptied a bag

Whether wearing conservative business suits or donning country garb for one of their extravaganzas, Penn and Teller's performances are always outrageous.

of cockroaches on the host. Another Letterman appearance introduced the illusionists' variation on a classic card trick: using giant, half-ton metal playing cards, they created a display of "sleight of forklift."

They starred in a public-television special, "Penn & Teller Go Public," and in several commercial-television specials. One of these, "Don't Try This at Home," featured Penn fulfilling a long-held fantasy: running over Teller with an eighteen-wheeler truck in front of New York's Radio City Music Hall.

They were closely involved with a PBS children's series, "Behind the Scenes," interviewing artists on their "tricks." Their 1989 feature-length movie, *Penn and Teller Get Killed*, was too gory to be a success with critics or audiences; more successful was an interactive computer video-game collection, *Smoke and Mirrors*, and books such as *How to Play in Traffic* and *How to Play with Your Food*.

They continue to perform live as well. They have a long-standing engagement at a casino in Las Vegas for several months each year. They make occasional national tours, such as the Refrigerator Tour, so called, Teller says, "because we open the show by dropping a refrigerator on our wretched selves." [115] And in the summer of 1998, they premiered their own weekly hourlong cable-TV series, *Penn & Teller's Sin City Spectacular*.

High-Tech Versus Skill

The illusionists' long-standing interest in high technology has led them into a continuing relationship with a group of scientists at the Massachusetts Institute of Technology (MIT). The object of the collaboration, they say, is simply to create "cool stuff." With these researchers, Penn and Teller have developed, among other things, a high-tech séance involving computerized music and delicate sensor instruments that enable the duo to detect invisible objects.

They stress, however, that high-tech gadgets are no substitute for expertise; as Penn puts it, technology "is just skill made of silicon":

> I think kids know just as much as I knew when I was a kid about what is difficult and what is beautiful and what is thought-provoking and what makes their heart sing with joy. When you are watching someone do a performance . . . it's only how they reach you. It's only that glimpse into another human being's heart that you want to see, and the technology is totally inert and separate from that, except to deliver to more and more people— more people can see Shakespeare now thanks to technology, but it doesn't change the writing. [116]

A scene from the gory 1989 movie Penn and Teller Get Killed. *Although the movie flopped with audiences and critics alike, Penn and Teller's video games and books have been well received.*

One aspect of their work that involves both high tech and skill is the issue of safety. Penn and Teller routinely play up the daredevil aspect of some of their stunts, and much of this is standard show-biz hype. There is also some genuine danger in what they do, however. For instance, when they perform their version of one classic act—catching speeding bullets in their teeth—they acknowledge that the trick has killed at least a dozen magicians throughout history.

However, Teller points out, he and Penn are fanatics for safety. "And because we're safety nuts," he says, "we're the ideal candidates to do something [genuinely dangerous]. We have survived because we have the same philosophy as Houdini: namely that we must pad every fatal trick with three levels of fail-safe." [117]

Still a Team

Since 1994, both illusionists have lived in Las Vegas, the magic capital of the world. Referring to the otherwordly nature of his adopted town, Teller says, "Life is my theme park. Why not live in one?" [118]

The two have occasionally done small projects individually— Teller has written on magic history, and Penn has made small appearances in films—but they remain firmly committed to working together. Still, they are partners more than friends, and, as with their onstage personas, the illusionists are in their personal lives a study in contrasts.

They do share certain traits. They are both atheists. They are both vehemently opposed to alcohol and drugs. They are both close to their parents, publicly showing great affection toward them, and in general they show only great respect toward older people. Penn does not see this as necessarily contrary to his other, more rebellious traits, confessing, "I like both kinds of people with blue hair."[119]

At the same time, they lead very different lives. Teller remains scholarly and introverted, living a reclusive private life.

In contrast, Penn is as outgoing in private life as on stage, having (among other things) dated a succession of glamorous women (one of whom, model Carol Perkins, appeared onstage to eat fire during one of the duo's tours). He relishes his lack of formal education and his lowbrow enthusiasms, which include Dean Martin, space launches, and Liberace.

Penn is content to live in a fairly modest home, close to the pair's Las Vegas office and its adjoining production warehouse. However, on a bluff outside the city, Teller is building himself a strange and elaborate mansion.

It is, he says, the fulfillment of boyhood treehouse fantasies he has had since he helped his parents build a tarpaper shack in rural Bucks County, Pennsylvania. Teller says his ultramodern, environmentally advanced house, when completed, will be "as sleekly industrial as Hoover Dam and as darkly goofy as Disney's Pirates of the Caribbean."[120]

Its design includes such touches as staircases hidden behind bookcases, phony optical-illusion windows, and more: "In the dining room, I'll have an electric chair you can sit in and shoot sparks from your fork. . . . I'll have window blinds fabricated from old X rays, and somewhere under the floor I'll be hiding an electromagnet whose purposes I'd rather not disclose."[121]

Magic's Future

The magicians and illusionists mentioned in this book are only a few of the countless performers who have entertained the world since the beginning of modern magic. The stories of other conjurors (including such luminaries as Gustavus Katterfelto, John Henry Anderson, Hofzinser, Buatier de Kolta, Frikell, Carter, Ching Ling Foo, P. T. Selbit, Raymond, and John Nevil Maske-

Prior to appearing on Bill Maher's late-night talk show, Penn chats with Craig Barrett of Intel. Although Penn and Teller are ardent supporters of technology, they maintain that high-tech innovations will never replace true skill.

lyne, the renowned grandfather of Jasper Maskelyne) are also as wonderful as the art to which they have devoted themselves.

Some of the best-known current stars, meanwhile, are Siegfried and Roy, Harry Blackstone Jr., Lance Burton, James Randi (the Amazing Randi), and Ricky Jay.

These performers, along with Copperfield and Penn and Teller, are working to make sure the art has a vivid future. As Milbourne and Maurine Christopher write of the future of magic, "Not for a moment do the contemporary masters believe the most illustrious pages in the history of magic belong to the past." [122]

NOTES

Introduction: Hocus Pocus!

1. Quoted in Roman Polanski, "The Most Popular Illusionist in the World," *Interview*, January 1996, p. 94.

2. Milbourne Christopher, *Panorama of Magic*. New York: Dover, 1962, p. v.

3. Kenneth Silverman, *Houdini!!!* New York: HarperCollins, 1996, p. 92.

4. Walter Gibson, *The Master Magicians*. Garden City, New York: Doubleday, 1966, p. 67.

5. Milbourne Christopher and Maurine Christopher, *The Illustrated History of Magic*. Portsmouth, NH: Heinemann, 1996, p. 198.

6. Gibson, *The Master Magicians*, p. 94.

7. Ruth Brandon, *The Life and Many Deaths of Harry Houdini*. New York: Random House, 1993, p. 315.

8. David Fisher, *The War Magician*. New York: Coward-McCann, 1983, p. 8.

9. Quoted in Calvin Trillin, *American Stories*. New York: Ticknor & Fields, 1991, p. 101.

10. Quoted in Trillin, *American Stories*, p. 101.

Chapter 1: Harnessing the Occult . . . Or Pretending To

11. Quoted in I. G. Edmonds, *The Magic Makers*. Nashville: Nelson, 1976, pp. 30–31.

12. Jasper Maskelyne, *Magic—Top Secret*. London: Stanley Paul & Co., 1947, p. 13.

13. Ricky Jay, *Learned Pigs and Fireproof Women*. New York: Villard Books, 1987, p. 85.

14. Quoted in Robert Hendrickson, *The Facts On File Encyclopedia of Word and Phrase Origins*. New York: Facts On File, 1977, p. 331.

15. Quoted in Jay, *Learned Pigs and Fireproof Women*, p. 20.

16. Christopher, *Panorama of Magic*, p. v.

17. Lisa Gubernick and Peter Newcomb, "Now You See It, Now You Don't," *Forbes*, September 27, 1993, p. 88+.

18. Quoted in press conference transcript (Penn and Teller), Ritz-Carlton Huntington Hotel, Pasadena, CA, July 12, 1998, p. 5.

19. Gibson, *The Master Magicians*, p. xv.

Chapter 2: Robert-Houdin: The Father of Modern Magic

20. Robert-Houdin, *Memoirs of Robert-Houdin*. New York: Dover, 1964, p. 5.

21. Robert-Houdin, *Memoirs of Robert-Houdin*, p. 18.

22. Robert-Houdin, *Memoirs of Robert-Houdin*, p. 22.

23. Quoted in Philip B. Kunhardt Jr., Philip B. Kunhardt III, and Peter W. Kunhardt, *P. T. Barnum: America's Greatest Showman*. New York: Knopf, 1995, p. 66.

24. Robert-Houdin, *Memoirs of Robert-Houdin*, pp. 99–100.

25. Quoted in Silverman, *Houdini!!!* p. 111.

26. Robert-Houdin, *Memoirs of Robert-Houdin*, pp. 158–59.

27. Robert-Houdin, *Memoirs of Robert-Houdin*, p. 294.

28. Quoted in Silverman, *Houdini!!!* p. 187.

Chapter 3: Herrmann the Great: The Devilish Magician

29. Christopher and Christopher, *The Illustrated History of Magic*, p. 187.

30. Gibson, *The Master Magicians*, p. 74.

31. Edmonds, *The Magic Makers*, p. 135.

32. Gibson, *The Master Magicians*, p. 84.

33. Christopher, *Panorama of Magic.* p. 131.

34. Christopher and Christopher, *The Illustrated History of Magic*, p. 196.

35. T. A. Waters, *The Encyclopedia of Magic and Magicians*. New York: Facts On File, 1988, p. 167.

Chapter 4: Kellar: The First Great American Magician

36. Gibson, *The Master Magicians*, p. 86.

37. Christopher and Christopher, *The Illustrated History of Magic*, p. 205.

38. Will Goldston, *Secrets of Famous Illusionists*. Ann Arbor, MI: Gryphon Books, 1971, p. 141.

39. Christopher, *Panorama of Magic*, p. 154.

40. Quoted in Christopher and Christopher, *The Illustrated History of Magic*, p. 208.

41. Quoted in Christopher, *Panorama of Magic*, p. 154.

42. Christopher, *Panorama of Magic*, p. vii.

43. Quoted in Gibson, *The Master Magicians*, p. 101.

44. Goldston, *Secrets of Famous Illusionists*, p. 142.

45. Christopher, *Panorama of Magic*, p. 159.

Chapter 5: Harry Houdini: King of Escapes

46. Quoted in Brandon, *The Life and Many Deaths of Harry Houdini*, p. 20.

47. Quoted in Milbourne Christopher, *Houdini: The Untold Story*. New York: Crowell, 1969, p. 13.

48. Brandon, *The Life and Many Deaths of Harry Houdini*, p. 44.

49. Quoted in William Lindsay Gresham, *Houdini: The Man Who Walked Through Walls*. New York: Holt, 1959, p. 75.

50. Quoted in Brandon, *The Life and Many Deaths of Harry Houdini*, p. 85.

51. Quoted in Christopher, *Houdini: The Untold Story*, pp. 50–51.

52. Quoted in Harold Kellock, *Houdini: His Life Story*. New York: Harcourt Brace, 1928, p. 56.

53. Brandon, *The Life and Many Deaths of Harry Houdini*, p. 213.

54. Quoted in Christopher, *Houdini: The Untold Story*, p. 154.

55. Walter B. Gibson, ed., *Houdini's Escapes and Magic*. New York: Funk and Wagnalls, 1930/reprinted 1976, p. 80.

56. Gresham, *Houdini: The Man Who Walked Through Walls*, p. 60.

57. Quoted in Brandon, *The Life and Many Deaths of Harry Houdini*, p. 292.

58. Quoted in Christopher, *Houdini: The Untold Story*, p. 260.

Chapter 6: Jasper Maskelyne: The War Magician

59. Maskelyne, *Magic—Top Secret*, p. 45.

60. Maskelyne, *Magic—Top Secret*, p. 16.

61. Quoted in Fisher, *The War Magician*, p. 12.

62. Maskelyne, *Magic—Top Secret*, p. 71.

63. Maskelyne, *Magic—Top Secret*, p. 30.

64. Maskelyne, *Magic—Top Secret*, p. 30.

65. Maskelyne, *Magic—Top Secret*, p. 53.

66. Quoted in Fisher, *The War Magician*, p. 85.

67. Quoted in Fisher, *The War Magician*, p. 207.

68. Maskelyne, *Magic—Top Secret*, p. 33.

69. Quoted in Fisher, *The War Magician*, p. 132.

70. Maskelyne, *Magic—Top Secret*, p. 155.

71. Quoted in Maskelyne, *Magic—Top Secret*, p. 65.

72. Quoted in Fisher, *The War Magician*, p. 312.

73. William Stevenson, *A Man Called Intrepid*. New York: Harcourt Brace Jovanovich, 1976, p. 190.

74. Maskelyne, *Magic—Top Secret*, p. 187.

Chapter 7: David Copperfield: "The First Pop Idol of Prestidigitation"

75. Gubernick and Newcomb, "Now You See It, Now You Don't," p. 88+.

76. Quoted in Gubernick and Newcomb, "Now You See It, Now You Don't," p. 88+.

77. Bill Zehme, "Shazam!" *Esquire*, April 1994, p. 90+.

78. Quoted in Polanski, "The Most Popular Illusionist in the World," p. 94+.

79. Quoted in Zehme, "Shazam!" p. 90+.

80. Quoted in Christopher and Christopher, *The Illustrated History of Magic*, p. 435.

81. Quoted in Zehme, "Shazam!" p. 90+.

82. Joanna Powell, "My Night with David Copperfield," *Good Housekeeping*, October 1996, p. 100+.

83. Waters, *The Encyclopedia of Magic and Magicians*, p. 87+.

84. Quoted in Polanski, "The Most Popular Illusionist in the World," p. 94+.

85. Quoted in Polanski, "The Most Popular Illusionist in the World," p. 94+.

86. Zehme, "Shazam!" p. 90+.

87. Quoted in Kim Cunningham, "Bat in the Hat," *People*, April 1, 1996, p. 114+.

88. Quoted in Powell, "My Night with David Copperfield," p. 100+.

89. Quoted in Joanna Powell, "The Nicest Cover Girl in the World," *Redbook*, July 1995, p. 66+.

90. Quoted in Powell, "My Night with David Copperfield," p. 100+.

91. *Time*, "Copperfield v. *Paris Match*," August 4, 1997, p. 74+.

92. Quoted in Doris Klein Bacon, "A Grand Illusionist, David Copperfield Shows the Ropes to Disabled Budding Magicians," *People*, April 18, 1983, p. 71+.

93. Quoted in Bacon, "A Grand Illusionist, David Copperfield Shows the Ropes to Disabled Budding Magicians," p. 71+.

94. Quoted in Gubernick and Newcomb, "Now You See It, Now You Don't," p. 88+.

95. Quoted in Zehme, "Shazam!" p. 90+.

96. Quoted in Gubernick and Newcomb, "Now You See It, Now You Don't," p. 88+.

97. Quoted in Polanski, "The Most Popular Illusionist in the World," p. 94+.

Chapter 8: Penn and Teller: "A Couple of Eccentric Guys Who Have Learned a Few Cool Things"

98. Trillin, *American Stories*, p. 102.

99. Quoted in Kathryn Bernheimer, "Enduring Duo Penn and Teller Have Been Reinventing Magic for 18 Years," Knight-Ridder/Tribune News Service, January 21, 1994, p. 0121+.

100. Quoted in Trillin, *American Stories*, p. 108.

101. Quoted in Pamela Miller, "Slightly Ajar," *Philadelphia*, December 1997, p. 131+.

102. Quoted in Trillin, *American Stories*, p. 133.

103. Quoted in press conference transcript (Penn and Teller), p. 4.

104. Quoted in Bernheimer, "Enduring Duo Penn and Teller Have Been Reinventing Magic for 18 Years," p. 0121+.

105. Quoted in Trillin, *American Stories*, p. 116.

106. Quoted in Trillin, *American Stories*, p. 127.

107. Quoted in Toby Kahn, "Magicians Penn and Teller Get No Sleight of Hand from Audience," *People*, September 2, 1985, p. 75+.

108. Quoted in Trillin, *American Stories*, p. 126.

109. Quoted in E. Graydon Carter, "Penn & Teller: Don't Call Them Magicians. They're Just 'A Couple of Eccentric Guys Who Have Learned to Do a Few Cool Things,'" *Life*, August 1985, p. 13+.

110. Charles Isherwood, "Penn & Teller," *Variety*, March 30, 1998, p. 172+.

111. Quoted in Bernheimer, "Enduring Duo Penn and Teller Have Been Reinventing Magic for 18 Years," p. 0121.

112. Trillin, *American Stories*, p. 119.

113. Quoted in press conference transcript (Penn and Teller), p. 10.

114. Edith Oliver, "Off Broadway," *New Yorker*, April 6, 1985, p. 125+.

115. Quoted in Trillin, *American Stories*, p. 292.

116. Quoted in press conference transcript (Penn and Teller), pp. 13–14.

117. Quoted in Jeff Rubio, "Penn and Teller—Faster than a Speeding Bullet?" *Orange County Register*, January 23, 1995, p. 12+.

118. Quoted in Miller, "Slightly Ajar," p. 166.

119. Quoted in Trillin, *American Stories*, p. 110.

120. Teller, "Mr. Teller Builds His Dream House," *GQ*, May 1997, p. 248.

121. Teller, "Mr. Teller Builds His Dream House," p. 249.

122. Christopher and Christopher, *The Illustrated History of Magic*, pp. 432–33.

Daniel Cohen, *Magicians, Wizards & Sorcerers*. Philadelphia: Lippincott, 1973. This book focuses on ancient wizards, sorcerers, and supposed psychics.

I. G. Edmonds, *The Magic Brothers*. New York: Elsevier/Nelson Books, 1979. Like Edmonds's other books (and many other biographies of the era), this work relies heavily on imagined conversation.

————, *The Magic Makers*. Nashville: Nelson, 1976. Profiles of famous illusionists, including the Herrmann Brothers and Robert-Houdin.

————, *The Magic Man*. Nashville: Nelson, 1972. A biography of Robert-Houdin, "the Father of Modern Magic."

William Lindsay Gresham, *Houdini: The Man Who Walked Through Walls*. New York: Holt, 1959. Although outdated by more current biographies, Gresham's book offers a glimpse into the life of Houdini.

Lace Kendall, *Masters of Magic*. Philadelphia: Macrae Smith, 1966. Chapters on many of the most famous magicians, including Robert-Houdin, Kellar, and Houdini. Contains at least one major error, referring to John Nevil Maskelyne throughout a chapter as "Jasper" (Jasper was J. N.'s grandson).

Joe Nickell, *Wonder-workers!* Buffalo, NY: Prometheus Books, 1991. A collection of profiles of psychics and illusionists, including Houdini and Robert-Houdin.

James Randi, *The Magic World of the Amazing Randi*. Holbrook, MA: Bob Adams Publishers, 1989. Simple magic tricks contributed by a number of contemporary magicians, with introductions by Randi.

WORKS CONSULTED

Books

Ruth Brandon, *The Life and Many Deaths of Harry Houdini*. New York: Random House, 1993. Perhaps the best of the many biographies written about the world's most famous magician.

Milbourne Christopher, *Houdini: The Untold Story*. New York: Crowell, 1969. Though superseded by subsequent biographies, this is still a classic.

——, *Panorama of Magic*. New York: Dover, 1962. A miscellaneous collection, with wonderful illustrations, of some of the more obscure corners of the magic world.

Milbourne Christopher and Maurine Christopher, *The Illustrated History of Magic*. Portsmouth, NH: Heinemann, 1996. This is a reprint of an excellent 1973 book by a well-known magician-writer, with a foreword by David Copperfield and additional chapters by Maurine Christopher.

David Fisher, *The War Magician*. New York: Coward-McCann, 1983. This story by a former reporter for *Life* magazine focuses on the wartime efforts of Jasper Maskelyne.

Walter B. Gibson, *The Master Magicians*. Garden City, NY: Doubleday, 1966. Profiles of some of the most famous illusionists, by a noted magician and writer on the subject.

——, ed., *Houdini's Escapes and Magic*. New York: Funk and Wagnalls, 1930. Reprinted 1976. A collection of Houdini's writings on magic.

Will Goldston, *Secrets of Famous Illusionists*. Ann Arbor, MI: Gryphon Books, 1971. A reprint of a 1931 book by a noted British magician.

Robert Hendrickson, *The Facts On File Encyclopedia of Word and Phrase Origins*. New York: Facts On File, 1977. A reference work on unusual words and phrases.

Ricky Jay, *Learned Pigs and Fireproof Women*. New York: Villard Books, 1987. Jay, a distinguished magician and scholar of magic, writes about unique and strange performers and their performances.

Harold Kellock, *Houdini: His Life Story*. New York: Harcourt Brace, 1928. This biography was published just two years after the illusionist's death.

Philip B. Kunhardt Jr., Philip B. Kunhardt III, and Peter W. Kunhardt, *P. T. Barnum: America's Greatest Showman.* New York: Knopf, 1995. A biography of the great American showman, with a few references to Robert-Houdin.

Jasper Maskelyne, *Magic—Top Secret.* London: Stanley Paul & Co., 1947. The long-out-of-print memoirs of the magician's exploits during World War II.

Robert-Houdin, *Memoirs of Robert-Houdin.* New York: Dover, 1964. This is a reprint of the famous conjuror's autobiography, translated by Lascelles Wraxall and first published in 1858.

Kenneth Silverman, *Houdini!!!* New York: HarperCollins, 1996. An excellent biography.

William Stevenson, *A Man Called Intrepid.* New York: Harcourt Brace Jovanovich, 1976. A book on secret Allied activity during World War II, with brief mentions of Jasper Maskelyne.

Calvin Trillin, "A Couple of Eccentric Guys," in *American Stories.* New York: Ticknor & Fields, 1991. Reprint of a lengthy profile of Penn and Teller that originally appeared in the *New Yorker* in 1989.

T. A. Waters, *The Encyclopedia of Magic and Magicians.* New York: Facts On File, 1988. A comprehensive volume with short entries on virtually every significant magician and magic term.

Periodicals

Doris Klein Bacon, "A Grand Illusionist, David Copperfield Shows Ropes to Disabled Budding Magicians," *People*, April 18, 1983.

Kathryn Bernheimer, "Enduring Duo Penn and Teller Have Been Reinventing Magic for 18 Years," Knight-Ridder/Tribune News Service, January 21, 1994.

E. Graydon Carter, "Penn & Teller; Don't Call Them Magicians. They're Just 'A Couple of Eccentric Guys Who Have Learned to Do a Few Cool Things,'" *Life*, August 1985.

Kim Cunningham, "Bat in the Hat," *People*, April 1, 1996.

Lisa Gubernick and Peter Newcomb, "Now You See It, Now You Don't," *Forbes*, September 27, 1993.

Charles Isherwood, "Penn & Teller," *Variety*, March 30, 1998.

Toby Kahn, "Magicians Penn and Teller Get No Sleight of Hand from Audiences," *People*, September 2, 1985.

Mimi Kramer, "Distractions," *New Yorker*, December 21, 1987.

Pamela Miller, "Slightly Ajar," *Philadelphia*, December 1997.

Edith Oliver, "Off Broadway," *New Yorker*, April 6, 1985.

Roman Polanski, "The Most Popular Illusionist in the World," *Interview*, January 1996.

Joanna Powell, "The Nicest Cover Girl in the World," *Redbook*, July 1995.

Joanna Powell, "My Night with David Copperfield," *Good Housekeeping*, October 1996.

Press conference transcript (Penn and Teller), Ritz-Carlton Huntington Hotel, Pasadena, CA, July 12, 1998.

Jeff Rubio, "Penn and Teller—Faster than a Speeding Bullet?" *Orange County Register*, January 23, 1995.

Teller, "Mr. Teller Builds His Dream House," *GQ*, May 1997.

Time, "Copperfield v. *Paris Match*," August 4, 1997.

Bill Zehme, "Shazam!" *Esquire*, April 1994.

INDEX

takes Alexander as apprentice, 36
tours with brother, 37
Herrmann, Leon (nephew of
Alexander and Carl), 43–44
Herrmann, Samuel (father), 36
Herrmann the Great. *See*
Herrmann, Alexander
Hilliard, John Northern
on Kellar, 53
Hitler, 72, 73, 77
is fooled by Magic Gang, 76
HMS *Hopeful*, 79
Hocus Pocus Junior (book), 21
Hocus Pocus Junior (magician), 22
Hofzinser, 25, 106
Honey Fitz (yacht), 89
Hoover, John Edgar, 64
Houdin, Josèphe (first wife of
Robert-Houdin), 28
Houdini, Harry, 12–13, 56, 83, 84,
102
childhood of, 57–58
death of, 14, 65–67
exaggerates effort to escape,
61–62
as friend of Kellar, 55
"gaffs" equipment, 63
is inspired by Robert-Houdin,
34, 58
makes movies, 63–64
meets Beatrice Raymond, 58
perfects Herrmann's brick wall
illusion, 38
runs away from home, 58
safety and, 105
self-promotion and, 12, 15
spiritualism and, 64–65
turns against Robert-Houdin, 35
Houdini Magical Hall of Fame, 68
How to Play in Traffic (Penn and
Teller), 104
How to Play with Your Food (Penn
and Teller), 104
Hughes, Isaiah Harris. *See* Fakir of
Ava

illusion, 9

Imam, 73
International Museum and Library
of the Conjuring Arts, 91
Isabella II, 36
Isherwood, Charles
on Penn and Teller, 102

Jay, Ricky, 21, 107
Jillette, Penn, 15
childhood of, 94–96
on Copperfield, 92
private life of, 105–106
see also Penn and Teller
Josef, Franz, 36

Katterfelto, Gustavus, 23, 106
Kellar, Harry, 12, 59, 84
adoption of, by Robert Harcourt,
45
apprenticeship of, at Dr. Squill's
Drugstore, 45
as assistant to Fakir of Ava, 45,
46, 47
death of, 56
death of Eva Medley and, 55
as first president of Society of
American Magicians (SAM),
54
looks for successor, 54–55
marries Eva Medley, 54
opens Kellar's Egyptian Hall, 54
performs after retirement, 56
prominence of, 44
purchases Buatier de Kolta's
illusion, 49–50
retires, 55
self-promotion and, 15
stage manner of, 12, 53
tours with William Fay, 48
works for Davenport Brothers,
48
Kellar's Egyptian Hall, 54
Kennedy, John F., 89
Kenya National Theatre, 82
Knievel, Evel, 98
Kolta, Buatier de, 106
Koontz, Dean, 91

PICTURE CREDITS

Cover photos: (background) Library of Congress, (clockwise from top, right) AP/Wide World Photos, Brown Brothers, AP Photo/Wally Fong, Brown Brothers

AP/Wide World Photos, 21, 101, 103, 107

Archive Photos, 18, 23, 90

Archive Photos/Saga/Frank Capri, 95

Brown Brothers, 37, 46

Corbis, 41, 80

Corbis/Michael Freeman, 91

Corbis/Hulton-Deutsch Collection, 14, 50, 70, 75, 76, 78

Corbis/Richard T. Nowitz, 93

Corbis/Neal Preston, 99

Corbis-Bettmann, 9, 25, 27, 29, 31, 32, 34, 39, 43, 44, 48, 52, 55, 66, 72

Express Newspapers/Archive Photos, 85

Fotos International/Archive Photos, 97, 105

FPG International, 62

Library of Congress, 11 (top), 13, 54, 63, 67

National Archives, 73

NBC-TV/Archive Photos, 84

© Pix Inc./FPG International, 59

Seth Poppel Yearbook Archives, 86

Popperfoto/Archive Photos, 57, 87

Stock Montage, Inc., 20

© Arthur Tilley/FPG International, 11 (bottom)

About the Author

Adam Woog is the author of many books for adults and young adults, including *The Importance of Harry Houdini* for Lucent Books. He lives in his hometown, Seattle, Washington, with his wife and young daughter.